"Change is hard. Change that happens because of a terrible tragedy is the worst kind of all. But Ken Roberts' story will remind you that anything is p   of book that will change your p   er struggle you're going throug   ur way out. My perspective ch   ng *Unexpected*, and there's no c   ."

Phil Cooke, Ph.D.
Filmmaker, media consultant, and author of *Jolt! Get the Jump on a World that's Constantly Changing*

"I wish we had published this book! Remarkably honest and thoughtfully delivered, Ken is one of those very rare voices who can speak with such clarity to the difficult topics of loss, pain, and confusion in life. He speaks to the issue from his own journey and the reader is not only endeared to the author for life, but will gain new insights that bring fresh hope through truth."

Jason Rovenstine
Publisher, Summerside Press

"I know Ken. I knew his dear wife Debbie. What I didn't know—until now—is the vast appreciation for life that Ken would glean from Debbie's sudden death. How fortunate for us that my friend has so masterfully woven vital life lessons together in this very winsome and readable volume. May *Unexpected* become the inspiring companion for you that it's already become for me."

John D. Beckett
CEO of Beckett Corporation and author of *Loving Monday and Mastering Monday.*

"There are some books that challenge us, others that inspire us; but, few books that profoundly discuss the reality of the piercing unexpected from a Christian perspective. Born out of personal experience, Ken Roberts has transparently, boldly, and poignantly presented the reader with an unabashed reason for hope and victory in the face of dire difficulties and painful uninvited events. This is a publication that I would consider to be an *essential* read for all who are willing to allow the Lord to etch within the soul HIS ultimate promise of *abundant life*, regardless of circumstances."

Glenn C. Burris, Jr.
President, The Foursquare Church

"I've watched Ken Roberts shepherd his family and his church through the trauma of losing his wife, my friend Debbie. His character, commitment, and wisdom can now be resources of the same for us through his new book, *Unexpected*. Thank you Ken, for helping us find our way via yours."

Lynette Lewis
author of *Climbing the Ladder in Stilettos*, speaker, business consultant

"Times of diversity and shattered dreams are when we most need God. Yet, those are the times we are most prone to question His power and goodness. Following a time of extreme loss, Ken Roberts shares his most intimate thoughts and feelings and openly discusses the real questions about God and how his own struggle resulted in a stronger faith and a reshaped spirit. His experience and insightful questions will be a great help to us all."

John K. Barnard
Executive Chairman
Vitamix Corp.

"Clearly written, thoughtfully described, this book draws hope from the ashes of personal devastation and the deepest kind of heartbreak. More than a book about shattered dreams and personal loss, Ken Roberts has skillfully made this a primer on spiritual formation. The author's unexpected tragedy becomes part of the fabric of spiritual formation in the heart of the reader."

Ron Roberts

Colonel, USAF, Retired

Northwest Airlines Executive

Pastor

"When I unexpectedly lost my wife, Ken's book became a source of life and light for my journey through grief and into recovery. In the months following my wife's death, I read many books on the topic of loss but found Ken's to be one-of-a-kind. Through reading *Unexpected* I learned to embrace my tragedy as an opportunity for personal transformation; found the right ways to feed my aching and empty soul and unlike any other book, *Unexpected* helped me experience healing, find hope and begin to dream again. It changed my perspective on living and I'm confident it will do the same for you."

Stephen Ekholm
Minister

Unexpected

Navigating Life's Unforeseen Turns

Ken L. Roberts

Unexpected
Navigating Life's Unforeseen Turns

Published by:
Intermedia Publishing, Inc.
P.O. Box 2825
Peoria, Arizona 85380
www.intermediapub.com

ISBN 978-1-937654-16-0

Dedication

To my parents—Rev. James and Joyce Roberts

> You have been an example to me in how to wisely navigate through life.

To my two children—Nicole and Britton

> I am so proud of who you have become and who you are becoming.

To my late wife—Debbie Tarsiuk Roberts

> Who through twenty-five years of life together, greatly shaped my life.

It is my deep desire, that by God's grace, I continue to wisely navigate through life and in the process become the person God has meant for me to be.

Ken L. Roberts

CONTENTS

CHAPTER ONE

Life Shatters

All love dies, only God's perfect love is eternal.

- C.S. Lewis

Everyone is on a journey. Everyone has a story. This is mine.

Tuesday, March 9, 2004 started out like any other day. I awoke around 6:30, anticipating the start of another day. I headed downstairs, put on the coffee, and waited for my wife to join me in the kitchen. Debbie and I grabbed our coffees, and moved into the living room to begin our usual morning routine: preparing for the activities of the day, planning our week, and simply being together. Our conversation drifted to our kids, current situations with friends, responsibilities at work, and thoughts of our future.

On this particular morning, our nineteen-year-old son interrupted our conversation, and asked his mom if she would come into his room to talk. This was very unusual. Britton, a late night person, was rarely awake at this time of the morning, much less initiating meaningful conversation. But sitting on the side of our son's bed, talking about topics he loved—music, movies, and sports—none of us knew how cherished this brief, unexpected, early morning exchange between mother and son would become.

Later, Debbie and I went back upstairs to our bedroom to get ready for the day. Exchanging our normal "I love yous" and a kiss, we said our goodbyes, and headed off in opposite directions.

I drove to the health club and like every other Tuesday morning, Debbie took our twenty-one-year-old daughter, Nicole, to her job. During their twenty-minute drive they listened to music, laughed, and talked about life in general. After dropping Nicole off at work, Debbie continued down the road to her women's Bible study group; just another routine drive, on another routine morning, at the start of another routine day.

I had just finished my workout, and was on my way home when my cell phone rang. On the other end of the line my daughter Nicole calmly informed me that the nearby hospital had just called her, trying to reach me. She said that Mom had been in a car accident. That's all she knew, she didn't have any details. So I didn't know if my wife had a few scratches, broken bones, or something worse.

Hurrying home, I picked up my son and rushed to the hospital emergency room. When we arrived, it was immediately clear that the situation was serious. Debbie had been broadsided on the driver's side of her car by a large sports utility vehicle. She was resuscitated at the scene of the accident and now in the emergency room lying unconscious in front of me.

I struggled to believe it. Tuesday, March 9, 2004, had started out like any other day, but, without warning, this journey called life took a sharp, unexpected turn. It would never be the same.

My wife's unresponsive body was promptly placed on a life-flight helicopter and transferred to the trauma unit of another area hospital. Once there, the waiting room rapidly filled with family, friends, and fellow workers, surrounding us with support, comfort, and prayers.

Within a few hours, the details of the accident were pieced together. Information from various sources—the two eyewitnesses, the EMTs, the attending police officers, the medical teams, and the neurologist's report, determined that while Debbie was driving to her women's Bible study group, she suffered a brain aneurysm, lost consciousness, and drove through a red light. At the same time, a young man on his way to work proceeded through the green light, hitting the driver's side of my wife's car, causing her severe brain damage. She was traveling south at only 35 mph; he was traveling east at only 25 mph. Not a high impact collision, but nonetheless, a life-shattering one.

Within the next twenty-four hours, it became brutally clear that my wife's brain damage was so severe she either needed a complete restorative miracle, or needed to graciously and mercifully pass. The other scenarios—living the rest of her life in a vegetative state, or my kids and I having to make the agonizing decision to take her off life support—were simply options that none of us wanted to face. One by one Debbie's vital organs began to shut down. My precious wife of twenty-five years, incredible mother of our two awesome kids, and wonderful friend to so many, at 12:40 p.m., Friday, March 12, 2004 was pronounced dead. She was only forty-seven years old.

Life happens. Life shatters.

CHAPTER TWO

Navigating Life

Teach me the lessons from living so I can stay the course.

- King David

A few years earlier I, too, thought I was about to die.

For several years, every fall I went whitewater rafting with a group of friends. This particular year, we traveled to Pennsylvania to raft down the Youghiogheny River. We arrived the night before, set up camp, built a fire, cooked our meal, and settled in around the campfire talking, laughing, and reminiscing.

Early the following morning we met our guides at our outrigging post, got our brief, whitewater rafting 101 instructions, divided up into four-man platoons, selected our rafts, and pushed off, gently meandering downstream.

The beginning of our trip was uneventful; peaceful and placid, bordering on boring. But, as we calmly floated down river we began to hear the sound of rushing rapids. Rounding a bend, looming right before us were level 5 whitewater rapids, roaring and raging—daring us to take them on. With a full adrenaline rush, my comrades and I plunged into the exploding water, our raft tossing and twisting like a rodeo cowboy on a bucking bronco.

As weekend adventure-seeking, middle-aged, suburban males, go, we were holding our own. As we rode our way through this wild water ride, we were manic; screaming from sheer panic one moment and laughing hysterically with unbridled joy the next. This was the adventure we came for. This was raw exhilaration. This was living.

I was perched on the side of the raft, yelling "yee haw," when without warning, we hit a large boulder hidden just beneath the foamy surface. The violent impact forced our rubber raft to make a sharp turn, and the momentum flipped me backwards, over the side and into the raging water. Stunned, I found myself in the most dangerous section of white water in the entire river and now at its mercy.

Recognizing the danger I was in, one of my rafting comrades impulsively jumped in to save me. Although his action was heroic, it was also extremely stupid. Now two of us were in serious peril.

After several minutes of frantic struggle, our rafting guides who had been following us in kayaks, arrived on the scene, threw us a rope and pulled us to shore. Irritated, they offered some advice for the next time we went overboard. "Did they say next time?" Then they rudely ordered us back into our raft and on with our journey. I coughed, wheezed, shivered, and coughed and wheezed some more. Finally, I caught my breath and calmed my nerves.

With far less male bravado than before, my friends and I floated downstream in silence. None of us knew exactly what was around the next bend, but we were all certain that at some point we would encounter white waters once again.

We've all been there: everything seems calm, meandering along with the day-to-day flow of life, and then without warning, we're flung into dangerous waters: a once healthy marriage crumbles, a son or daughter becomes an addict, a long friendship abruptly ends, a parent's health quickly declines, a business investment goes bad, a routine check-up reveals cancer, a long-awaited child is born deformed.

Adversity doesn't discriminate. Live life long enough and unexpected turns happen to all of us. One moment we find ourselves merrily floating downstream and the next we are violently tossed into the raging waters of life, shocked, shivering, and shaking. Eventually, we fight our way back into the raft and our journey continues. But uneasiness remains, and wariness lingers, reminding us that at some point, around another bend, perhaps another patch of white water awaits us.

———————

I wrote *Unexpected* because of an unforeseen turn in my own life. My wife's death launched me on a quest, forcing me to face some central questions about the ways of God and the meaning of life. In my search, other related and vital questions also emerged. Was I becoming the person I was meant to be, or because of the difficulties and disappointments of life had another person, a stranger, emerged? Was I living life with passion and purpose or had the predictability of life lulled me into merely existing? Was I fulfilling what I was designed and destined for or had I drifted off course, aimlessly floating along?

Over the years, I've often been inspired by the words of Henry David Thoreau: "I went to the woods because I wished to live deliberately... and not when I came to die, discover I had not lived." [1] With my wife's passing I knew it was time for me to put these poignant and penetrating words into action.

As a way to wrestle with perplexing questions and unpack the painful emotions left in the wake of my tragedy, I began to journal. What started as a few raw and scattered entries, over time emerged as the core ideas for *Unexpected: Navigating Life's Unforeseen Turns.*

Let me be clear—this book is not about death, it's about life! If you've drifted away from your chosen destination, I trust this book will help you make the needed course corrections and return to a life of purpose. If the routine of life has put you in mere survival mode, I hope this book will help you return to a life of passion. And most importantly to me, if you've experienced an unexpected turn in life, I sincerely desire that *Unexpected: Navigating Life's Unforeseen Turns* will help you wisely traverse through it, and in the process, become the person you were meant to be.

To get the most out of this book, I would suggest you take the time to consider the reflection/discussion questions found at the end of each chapter. It may be helpful to read through *Unexpected* the first time without answering these questions. And then read the book a second time and work through these questions. You may also consider reading the book and working through the reflection/discussion sections with some friends, a book reading club, or a small group from your church. Whatever way you decide to proceed through this book, you will get the most out of your time by applying the lessons shared in this book, through the grid of our own life and story.

Many centuries ago, one of the great wisdom writers described the importance of wisely navigating life with these prayerful words, "God, teach me the lessons from living so I can stay the course." [2]

This book is an invitation to an expedition; an exploration into your life and mine.

So get in. Grab an oar. Let's start rowing.

Reflection/Discussion Questions

1. What unforeseen turns have you experienced in your life?

2. Did you navigate through these times in ways that moved you toward who you hope to become?

3. Are you currently experiencing an unforeseen turn in your life?

4. If so, are you navigating through it in a way that is moving you toward, or away from who you hope to become?

5. In the midst of both the demands and routine of life, are you becoming the person you were meant to be? If not, why?

6. Are you living life with passion and purpose? If not, why?

7. Are you fulfilling what you were designed and destined for? If not, why?

CHAPTER THREE

Lingering Questions

Asking "why" does not mean we have lost our faith, rather a sign of faith.

- Ruth Graham

For weeks after my wife's death, I found myself emotionally and physically depleted, stumbling through each day. Dealing with the endless details of burial plots, medical bills, and insurance documents, not to mention my newly inherited domestic chores of paying bills, buying groceries, making beds, washing dishes, doing laundry, cleaning the house—were staggering, but nonetheless, the duties kept me occupied and somewhat distracted from the constant grief. I wanted to close the doors, pull the blinds, crawl under the covers, shut down, and give up. I wanted to tell life to "go away." But it didn't; it wouldn't. Even though I felt dead, the world and life around me moved on.

Although these first months were extremely difficult, I found solace in a new friend and was carried along from a source beyond. From my religious training, I knew that this invisible strength was called *grace*. Through grace, God enables the weak to do what they can't do on their own. And finding myself in a place that I had never been before—broken and bruised—I warmly welcomed grace into my life. On days when it seemed I could not go on, like a father carrying his injured child, God's strength came and carried me. At times, when I was too weak to even make the request, grace came softly rushing in. My new friendship with grace, found and forged during this fragile time in my life, still remains with me today.

Five months after Debbie's passing, I experienced a noticeable shift in my journey. Memories of our twenty-seven years of a beautiful and cherished life came racing back, flooding my mind, tearing my soul. Places we had been, experiences we had shared, conversations we had exchanged, and dreams we had dreamed. The memories were precious, yet painful. The longer my wife was gone, the deeper and more permanent the feelings of loss penetrated me. My emotions were not as raw or openly exposed as they were at first, but at times the feelings still left me numb, and at other times they left me overwhelmed and crushed. The reality of the long-term effect Debbie's absence would have upon me, my two kids, my extended family, and her many close friends slowly settled in like a heavy fog.

Along with the memories came the inevitable questions. Why did this happen? Why did God allow this? Did He allow it? Where was God? Where *is* God?

These perplexing questions, like a stuck record, played over and over in my head, each time evoking painful emotions. Sometimes the feelings were turbulent; churning, erupting, and exploding. At other times, like ominous, darkening storm clouds, the feelings persistently lingered, taking up residence inside of me. I felt self-pity and abandonment, defiance and anger. I experienced a sense of injustice and resentment. I felt fear and futility concerning my future. My emotions, like a band of mustangs on the open range, ran wild, screaming, "It isn't fair! It doesn't make sense. Why me? What did I do to deserve this?"

Ruth Graham, a fellow traveler struggling with her own questions in response to tragedy, adequately expressed my own, when she wrote, "Asking 'why' does not mean we have lost our faith. Asking why can be, rather a sign of faith. When we ask why, we are asserting our desire to dialogue with the God in whom we have put a measure of trust. We expect he is listening and believe he is the source of the answers. God is not threatened by our emotions. He is not shaken by our 'why?' He invites honesty." [1]

Victor Frankl, a Holocaust survivor and noted psychotherapist, maintained that people could endure any "what" as long as they have a "why." [2] For my own sanity, I realized I too needed to find some reasonable answers to my "why" questions.

Life's lingering questions are certainly not easy to resolve. When faced with tragedy, many of us avoid going to the mental and emotional depths that exploring these difficult questions demand. In an effort to cope, some simply avoid the questions while others conveniently submerge or sedate their emotions. Ultimately, neither option is satisfactory.

These demanding questions and damaged emotions left unresolved, like a beach ball being held under the water, will eventually resurface. Either the experience of another unexpected tragedy or the accumulation of life's disappointments will cause the same questions and emotions to come surging back, often with more destructive force than before. Try as we may, there is just no way to keep them submerged forever.

Recently I spoke with a young man who as a child tragically lost his brother. Now, as his mother lies in a coma after a routine hospital procedure, he once again faces the same familiar questions and overwhelming emotions he felt twenty years earlier. With these questions unaddressed and our emotions unattended we are left unprepared and vulnerable on the next leg of our journey.

Dr. Larry Crabb, a noted Christian psychologist, observes that during times of tragedy "countless numbers of people quietly dismiss God and learn to live like functional atheists or pragmatic deists." With what appears to be God's absence during their tragedy they resolve, "There is no God I can depend on. The God who exists has left me to make it on my own. He offers no real help." He finishes his quote with these sad but true words, "Too many churches are filled with worshipers who have come to this conclusion." [3]

I was determined not to become one of those statistics. I refused to naively believe that over time the wounds on my soul would magically disappear. I refused to conveniently settle for prepackaged theological propositions or swallow shallow spiritualized theories. I refused to submerge my hurt and pain or be held captive by my rogue runaway emotions. I refused to become a passive victim of tragedy. Somehow, I had to find sufficient answers to my unanswered questions and find healing for my shattered soul. I knew the health of my future journey depended upon it.

Each of us is on our own unique journey. Mine may be different from yours, yet inevitably the tragic events we experience in life leave all of us with lingering questions and scarred emotions.

In the following chapters, I'll share with you how, over time, I navigated through my own questions, found healing for my wounded soul, and in the process moved toward the person I was meant to be.

But before we get to that part of the journey, let me share with you how I dealt with the following question: "What do we do with shattered dreams left in the wake of the unexpected turns in life?"

Reflection/Discussion Questions

1. As a result of some of the unforeseen turns in your own life, or those you've seen other people experience, what are some of your lingering questions?

2. Do you agree or disagree with Ruth Graham's quote, "Asking 'why' does not mean we have lost our faith rather {it is} a sign of faith?"

3. Due to any unexpected turns in your life, are you (or have you) avoiding exploring some of your lingering questions? If so, what are the questions and why are you avoiding them?

4. Due to an unforeseen event in your life, are you (or have you) submerging or sedating any of your emotions left in the wake of that event? If so, which emotions and why and how are you submerging or sedating them?

5. During any of those unforeseen turns in your life, have you experienced a new understanding of God's grace? If so, how?

6. Are you currently living your life either as a functional atheist or pragmatic deists? (i.e. believing or feeling that God is not interested or involved in situations you are facing in your own life.)

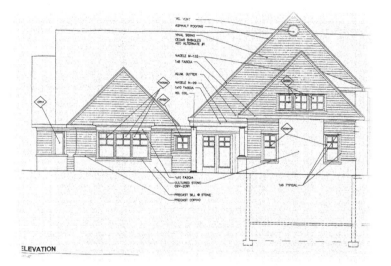

RG. VENT
ASPHALT ROOFING

VINAL SIDING
CEDAR SHINGLES
ADD ALTERNATE #1

NAGELE M—132
1x8 FASCIA

ALUM. GUTTER
NAGELE M—99
1x10 FASCIA
WD. COL.

1x10 FASCIA
CULTURED STONE
CSV—2091

PRECAST SILL @ STONE
PRECAST COPING

1x6 TYPICAL

ELEVATION

CHAPTER FOUR

Shattered Dreams

Dreams can be the greatest source of our pleasure or the greatest source of our pain.

- Ken L. Roberts

Debbie and I were dreamers.

One of our many dreams was to have a "hospitality house." We often talked about building a large, spacious home where people with various interests—artists, musicians, writers, designers, engineers, architects—would gather, engage in stimulating conversations and in the process develop deep, lasting friendships. We envisioned people from all walks of life—whether from around the world or just down the street—relaxing in a comfortable Great room, with an inviting fire blazing in the stone fireplace, discussing theology, philosophy, history, culture, art, and music. This dream deeply motivated us.

Debbie and I set our hopes on a beautifully wooded lot in an ideal location near our new church facility. One particular day, as we were overcome with "dream fever," we decided to once again cruise by and case out our desired property. We drove up and down the street several times, drawing suspicious looks from the neighbors, and finally mustered up enough nerve to actually stop and take a closer look. Like two burglars making an unauthorized entry, we parked the car and apprehensively yet excitedly stepped onto the property. As we walked, ideas streamed out. With every forbidden step Debbie and I giddily created our dream home. We talked about what the house would look like, how we would decorate it, who the first guests would be, and what interesting subjects would be discussed. At that moment our hospitality house seemed like a reality, completely within our grasp.

Coincidentally, the owners of the lot were members of the church where I pastored. And a few weeks after our trespassing outing, one Sunday after church we unexpectedly found ourselves having lunch together. The lot wasn't up for sale and we had no idea what they were planning to do with it, so when the topic of our dream house surfaced during our conversation, we sheepishly asked if they would consider selling it to us. They appeared surprised by our request, but said they would think about it and let us know. A few months went by without any word, until one Saturday evening, we were all in attendance at a wedding of a mutual friend. During the reception the owners of the lot pulled us aside, and with big smiles on their faces, told us they had talked it over and decided to give us the lot! (Yes, you read that right—*give us the lot*.) Completely taken aback, like two children on Christmas morning, our mouths dropped open and our hearts leapt. We were overjoyed.

With new energy, Debbie and I began making plans for our new home. First we contacted a gifted architect, who was also a friend, and after only a few brief meetings, the perfect architectural plan for our "hospitality house" was complete. Then another surprise. Our architect informed us that his time and services on our project would be donated— completely free! The quick pace and utter generosity reaffirmed our feeling that our project was blessed and meant to be.

Next, we selected a trusted and talented contractor; also a long-time friend. He enthusiastically agreed to build our home and immediately, along with our architect, began working on the blueprints, sending out and securing bids, preparing a budget, and scheduling a start date. Everything was moving forward. We were set to build... .

And then, my wife's accident and death.

How does one deal with shattered dreams—especially dreams we thought were initiated by God? It's one thing to deal with dreams of our own making, which come to an end. It's quite another to understand why dreams die that we sincerely believed God was backing.

In the months following Debbie's death, how to navigate through shattered dreams and unfulfilled promises became one of the most disturbing questions for me. It seemed that with my wife's passing the dam broke, and all the unfulfilled dreams accumulated on my journey over the years, flooded in.

We had just recently moved our church congregation into a new facility, which was a dream of ours for almost twenty years.

And then, my wife's accident and death.

Debbie had just started a new business that held great potential and promise, fulfilling one of her cherished dreams.

And then, her accident and death.

With our two children now grown, we were looking forward to sharing the next season of our life together.

And then, her accident and death.

Debbie and I had battled for years to see many of our dreams come to pass, and many of them seemed so close, just within our grasp, but now they were shattered, gone. The battle fatigue from long fought for, yet unfulfilled promises, like a soldier worn and weary from war, finally took its toll. My heart was left crushed and cold.

In an effort to console me and explain away my unfulfilled promises, many people offered religious formulas, others concocted super-spiritualized theories, and still others fabricated mystical spins. These well-intended, but feeble attempts to explain the mysteries left in the wake of my tragedy were completely unsatisfactory. And at times they even felt utterly cruel. In my state of deep grief, no matter from which angle I viewed my situation, I was unable to make sense of any of it. To me the stark reality remained, my dreams had been stolen and the promises broken.

My struggle wasn't with the character of God. I still believed in His goodness and still embraced the truth that He rules over all things. I accepted the reality that His wisdom was far beyond my own. In fact, the assurance in God's promise of salvation and eternal life were now more real and secure to me than ever. My wife's passing hadn't weakened these long-held beliefs, only strengthened them.

I did struggle however, with the ways of God. They just didn't make sense. I didn't understand what appeared to be God's lack of interest and involvement concerning His promises to me in this present life. Psychologist Dr. Larry Crabb summed up my exact feelings when he wrote, "Are we expected to experience God as unresponsive to our well-being and pretend we like Him anyway? Things that matter deeply to us don't seem to matter to Him. What are we to do with that fact? I find it hard to take comfort in God's commitment to his own glory when it doesn't seem to involve enough interest in me." [1]

As I sifted through my shattered dreams, I began asking the same question that another Christ follower had voiced centuries before, "Lord we have left everything to follow you, what benefit do we get *in this life* in return?" [2] The tangible rewards from years of faithfully following Christ seemed to be eluding me. God's ways left me confused and disillusioned. It felt like He was ignoring me, or even worse, abandoning me. I felt alone, befriended only by fatalism and futility.

For many of us, when we assess the ways of God, we often conclude that the math doesn't work. In our equation, God's promise to us, *plus* our obedience to Him, should *equal* the fulfillment of that promise. To us, this is how it should add up. But in reality how many times have we thought we heard from God, stepped out in faith, and instead of experiencing the fulfillment and reward just the opposite occurs? In obedience, we walk out on a limb and someone (it seems like that someone is God) begins to suddenly saw the limb off behind us, leaving us precariously dangling for our very life.

Let me be clear. I am aware that we have an enemy who opposes God's promises for our lives. I do understand there is resistance to the fulfillment of God-given dreams. I do realize that perseverance and patience are essential ingredients for promises to be obtained. I understand these things. However, as we faithfully follow God, there is an expectation that at some point, in some definable and tangible way, we will receive the promises (even if only partially) in the here and now. When this doesn't happen, it leaves us disillusioned and defiant with the ways of God, limping along, feeling wounded and betrayed by the very One we have attempted to faithfully trust and follow.

In these first few chapters, I've attempted to present some of the difficult questions we all face through life:

> What do we do when unexpected turns happen in life?

> How do we deal with some of life's lingering questions left in the wake of difficulty and disappointments?

> What do we do with shattered dreams and unfulfilled promises?

In the next several chapters, I will share with you some of the ways that I navigated through these questions. My hope is that as we move through the remainder of this book, you will somehow make sense of the inevitable and unforeseen turns of life, and in the process, move toward the person you were meant to be.

Our journey isn't over. So let's continue to row.

Reflection/Discussion Questions

1. Are there areas in your life where your once greatest source of pleasure has become your greatest source of pain? If yes, what are they?

2. Are you aware of any dreams that at one time you felt were inspired by God but now they seem to be aborted or abandoned? If so, what are they?

3. Do you struggle with the character of God?

4. Do you struggle with the "ways of God?"

5. Do you sometimes wonder if there are any tangible rewards experienced in this life for following God? If so, what are they? If not, why?

CHAPTER FIVE

Solid Footing

I'll huff, and I'll puff, and I'll blow your house down.

- The Big Bad Wolf

The wise man built his house upon the rock.

- Jesus

In 2002, the church I pastored began construction on a new facility and during excavation engineers discovered that the building site was located on a bed of shale. The construction company and architectural firm determined the best solution was to drill through the thin layers of shale until they reached solid rock. Holes were drilled around the building's perimeter, eight to ten feet deep and filled with concrete. Then, a block wall was built on top of the pylons, establishing a solid base sufficient to support the building's massive weight.

From the outside of the building you could see some of the block foundation, but the pylons which the block foundation rested upon weren't visible at all. Most people who walked through the facility often commented about the size of the building, or admired the scenic view through the spacious glass atrium. Others were impressed with the thirty-foot-high wood panels in the auditorium, or appreciated the masterful masonry throughout the building. But I never heard even one person mention the concrete pylons that held up the entire building, located just inches beneath their feet.

In the months following my wife's death, with my perplexing questions unanswered and painful emotions surging, I felt as though I was standing in the middle of a rapidly rising river, the swift current threatening to sweep my feet out from under me. I needed to get to safety and regain some solid footing. I needed to revisit the foundations of my faith.

The first foundation I revisited was my belief that God is God and I am not. I simply, yet firmly, made a decision to re-embrace the fact that God was *still* God in my life. This was not, by any means, what my feelings were telling me to do. Like a spoiled child throwing a tantrum in the middle of a toy store, my emotions were screaming, "This isn't fair! I don't deserve this! I have every right to be angry with God!" Even so, I resolved that I would not be led by my unruly emotions, but rather be led by my convictions about God. Reestablishing my previous worldview that *He is God and I am not*, became the starting point and my ongoing chart for navigating through this tumultuous period in my life.

We all come to a point in our personal journey when we must choose who our god is. For a follower of Christ, the reality of this choice is most deeply tested during a time of adversity. It's when it seems that God isn't really in control, and we question His goodness toward us, that our faithfulness to Him is most intensely challenged. When things happen that don't make sense, or things go contrary to our desires, will we continue to trust God? That's the test. It is one thing to subscribe to a theology that God is by his very nature good and rules over all things, it's quite another to embrace this belief as a reality in the midst of our own difficulties and devastations.

For those who hold a worldview other than Christianity, an answer to the question, "Who is our god?" is still required. As Bob Dylan popularized in a song years ago, "We *all* have to serve somebody." The options are limited. We can choose to trust in ourselves, convincing ourselves that through the accumulation of position, power, or wealth, we can storm proof our lives. Or, we can choose to believe that by our own strength, ingenuity, and cleverness we can maneuver through whatever life might bring our way.

Another option is to trust in others. This choice leads us to rely on our spouse, family, friends, religion, or other man-made systems. Although these relationships or institutions may be dependable, they were never intended to be our primary source of reliance. Man-made systems inevitably fail us. And, people make wonderful relationships—but they make terrible gods.

We can trust in ourselves, trust in others, or trust in God. These are the three options available to us, but ultimately we are all forced to choose one. Like the foundations of a Manhattan skyscraper, getting this issue right from the start has huge implications. *Who we choose to rely on during difficult times along our journey sets the foundation and becomes the central compass from which we navigate through all of life.*

Each of us, at times, is tempted to create gods according to our own preference. Deep down, we all desire a god who would fashion for us a perfect life in a perfect world. If we could, we would program him (or her) to govern the universe according to our design. This customized arrangement can be made with a god but cannot be made with the one true God.

I'm not suggesting a simplistic, Pollyanna approach to the hard issues of life, nor am I promoting a naïve and passive "whatever will be, will be" outlook to life. I'm not suggesting a blind and thoughtless faith, nor am I promoting prepackaged religious remedies. Trusting in God does not mean we are reduced to mindless robots.

What I am suggesting, however, is that trying to comprehend and control things in our life *on our own* is comparable to a second grader designing, assembling, and flying the space shuttle. It's absurd and impossible. And when we do foolishly attempt it, inevitably it ends in disaster.

Many of our obsessions and addictions—whether sex, money, drugs, pleasure, power, position, relationships, religion, or whatever they may be—are often the result of our search for and reliance upon insufficient gods. What I've discovered in my own life, is that who or what I run to for strength and solace during times of discomfort and difficulty, uncovers my idols and reveals my true gods: a late-night ice cream indulgence when I'm depressed, spending money on things I don't need, when I'm sad, or a television binge when I'm stressed. Whatever they may be, we all have our favorite gods.

For those of us who embrace the God of the Bible as the One who governs the universe and oversees the details of our life, the following words directly apply, "We will come to a point in our personal struggle when we must make the decision either to trust God or disbelieve him. By choosing to trust him, we make our peace with him." [1]

Since I felt that God had allowed this tragedy to occur in my life, after losing Debbie, I found it difficult to pray. My once intimate friendship with God was now fractured and frail. Personal and detailed conversations with God weren't something at the time I had any interest in. I felt deeply betrayed by the very One I had passionately loved and faithfully followed. Why would I want to talk with him now!

But even though I found it difficult to pray, I did not find it difficult to worship. And therefore one of the ways that I chose to express my trust in God after my wife's death was through personal worship. In fact, I experienced great comfort and healing during these times. Due to my theological training, I knew that one of the primary ideas for worship in the Bible presents the image of bowing before a king. I was well aware that the Bible was full of stories of men and women who throughout their journey, as an expression of surrender, learned to bow before God; some willingly, some reluctantly. Abraham, after many years of journeying with God, learned to bow. Moses, after a lengthy road trip in the desert arranged by God, learned to bow. Daniel's three friends, facing execution by fire, refused to bow to a foreign god, but instead, willingly bowed to the one true God. Even Jacob, a man whose entire life had been bent on getting his own way, after a long night of wrestling with God, broke and eventually bowed.

During the months after Debbie's passing, this aspect of worship—the act of bowing—became the guiding posture of my heart toward God. Although I did not understand God's ways, nor was I pleased with His ways, yet like a subject before His king, I still willingly chose to bow.

I've stood in the front row at church, literally hundreds of times, singing with gusto…

Take my life and let it be,

consecrated Lord to Thee,

On other occasions I've stood with my hands raised and tears streaming down my face singing…

I surrender all, I surrender all

All to Thee my blessed savior

I surrender all.

Although I had sung about surrender, and even preached on it many times, until this tragedy occurred in my life, I didn't even vaguely understand what it meant to surrender. But all that changed on the evening of my wife's death.

All throughout the day of Debbie's passing, family and friends arrived at the hospital to express their sorrow and extend their support. Later that night I drove home with my two children and somewhere along the way, the three of us began to talk about Mom. When we arrived at our house, I parked in the driveway, turned the car off, and our tender conversation about "Mom" continued. As we talked in our pain and through our tears, we unexpectedly (and miraculously) stumbled upon two specific things in our conversation that would profoundly affect how we would navigate through this season of our life.

The first thing we talked about was that since *one of the four of us had departed early, we were grateful Mom got to go home first.* Although devastated by her passing, we were thankful she wasn't the one who had to stay behind and bear the pain that we were currently experiencing. Even with our hearts aching, we each commented how we *felt honored to remain behind, continue to navigate through life the best we could and faithfully await the day the four of us would once again be reunited.*

As the conversation continued, the second thing that occurred was that the three of us accepted her passing. We openly discussed the shocking realization that we could not change the fact that she was gone, and understood to deny the reality of her death would be foolish and futile. Remarkably, at that very moment, in the midst of our deep pain and heavy sorrow, each one of us willingly chose to embrace "Mom's passing" as forever part of our story. Even though today Nicole, Britton, and I still feel the pain of our loss, our deliberate decision on that night to embrace the tragedy, no doubt has helped us journey on with meaningful lives—although at times we still walk with a noticeable limp.

In the midst of surrendering my wife's passing to a good and caring God, I stumbled upon an unexpected gift. It was like opening a clenched fist full of sand, so that a precious pearl could be put in its place. Instead of fighting with life,

I learned to embrace it and by embracing life, I began to experience a more abundant life. Things that once easily irritated and even angered me, no longer did. Things I had excessively worried about, I no longer did. When I abandoned my own will and readily embraced God's goodness and faithfulness in the midst of my tragedy, I gained a dimension of joy, peace, and freedom I had never experienced before.

These words written by one of my mentors, Dallas Willard, describes my own experience well,

What remarkable changes this [surrender] introduces into our day-to-day life! Personally, at the beginning of my day—often before arising—I commit my day to the Lord's care. Then I meet everything that happens as sent or at least permitted by God. I meet it resting in the hand of his care. This helps me to "do all things without grumbling or disputing" (Phil. 2:14), because I have already placed God in charge and am trusting him to manage them for my good. I no longer have to manage the weather, airplanes and other people. Trusting in God's care frees us from the burden of looking out for ourselves." [2]

I'm not suggesting the *process* of surrender is easy or instantaneous. It's not. We still experience the continued resistance from our emotions and the ongoing revolts of our will. Just as leaning back and pushing your body *away* from the wall while rock repelling is counterintuitive, so are the initial feelings of surrendering the details of our life to God. Control isn't something we easily relinquish. As we continue to practice a life of surrender, however, we don't lose our life, we find it. Or as one man I read about, who was slowly dying from Lou Gehrig's Disease, insightfully put it, "Once you learn how to die (surrender), *then* you learn how to live." [3] Jesus said the same thing yet another way, "Whoever aims to save their life shall lose it, but whoever loses their life for my sake shall find it." [4]

Looking back over the years since my wife's death, I now realize that the most important decision I made in the early stages of my restorative process was to stand firm on the fact that God is God and I am not. And to Him, I chose to bow. For me, this decision became the anchor from which every other decision was tethered. I believe this foundation is not only *one* of the central issues in learning to navigate wisely through life, but *the* central issue. Without it, we are left vulnerable, adrift, and tossed by the unexpected turns in life.

None of us can know just how much weight the demands and difficulties of life might one day be placed upon the foundations of our faith, nor are we even sure our foundations can carry the weight. I'm no longer the pastor of the congregation who owns that beautiful and massive building, but I do know the building still stands. I do know the pylons work.

Reflection/Discussion Questions

1. Do you believe that God is in control of all things? If not, why? If so, why is there so much tragedy and pain in life?

2. Ultimately who or what do you put your trust in? God—Yourself—Others

3. List some of your own idols (i.e. things that you run to for strength and solace during times of discomfort or difficulty).

4. In the midst of your unexpected turn(s) in life, are you still worshipping (bowing to God)? (i.e. acknowledging that He is God and you are not.)

5. Have you loosened your grip (control) of the situation and are you surrendering it to God?

6. At the beginning of each day are you able to commit your day to the Lord's care and as a result, embrace the things that come your way throughout the day as things already in His awareness and under His care and control?

CHAPTER SIX

A Costly Life

Come, follow me and I will give you life.

-Jesus

I became a follower of Jesus at a very young age. When I was six my dad decided to become a pastor. To start his new career, Dad quit his blue-collar job, sold the little house where we lived in Michigan, paid off our debts, loaded our family and furniture into a truck and moved us 600 miles south. The church in Tennessee that had elected my dad as their new pastor had about thirty members and generously promised to pay him $50 a week—*if* it came in the offering. It was in my dad's little church on a Sunday night, at the age of seven, that I made a decision to follow Christ. And I have been a faithful follower ever since.

I've spent the last forty years diligently practicing "spiritual disciplines:" praying, reading the Bible, worshipping, witnessing, journaling, fasting, serving, and giving. I've dutifully attended endless church activities: Sunday school classes, church camps, kids clubs, youth meetings, Bible studies, prayer meetings, revival services, choir practices, board meetings, conferences, retreats, seminars….

And one of the things I've noticed about my spiritual journey over these past years is that the longer I go the more baggage I tend to accumulate. Like an inexperienced hiker cramming too much stuff in my backpack, the accumulation of "spiritual disciplines" and church activities, although intended to be useful, ultimately catch up to us, leaving us weighted down and weary. I wonder just how much progress Pilgrim would have made on his journey to the Celestial City, if he'd been lugging all the stuff Christians currently are expected to carry in our knapsacks?

I totally identify with the Christian leader Ruth Haley Barton, as she writes of her own weariness caused by excessive Christian activities.

> Years ago, I sat in a staff meeting at a church I was serving; the purpose of the meeting was to talk about how we could attract more people to join the church. At one point someone counted the requirements for church membership that were already in place and made the startling discovery that somewhere between five and nine commitments *per week* were required of those who wanted to become church members! Outwardly I tried to be supportive of the purpose of the meeting, but on the inside I was screaming, *Who would want to sign up for this?* I was already becoming aware of my Christian fatigue syndrome in my own life and couldn't imagine willingly inflicting it on someone else. [1] (author's emphasis)

To a Christ follower, Christian activities disconnected from the source, the person of Jesus Christ, quickly decline into drudgery and demands. No matter how creatively it's labeled or how cleverly it's camouflaged, the result of religion is always the same; it leaves us weary and worn out, disappointed and disillusioned. What was once fresh becomes stale. What was once passionate becomes boring. What was once invigorating becomes suffocating. Religion is like a marriage that remains only because of vows spoken years earlier, even though the intimacy and authenticity of the relationship has long since dissolved. On the outside we still act the part, but on the inside, life has already moved out and only a hollow shell remains; leaving duty instead of devotion, routine instead of relationship, activity instead of adventure.

With the weight of my wife's death, I was convinced neither spiritual disciplines nor church activities, *alone,* could sustain me. It's not that these activities were no longer important to my life, it was just that they had become extremely heavy. Engaging in these activities must be the *result* of or *assistance* to our ongoing, personal, and authentic relationship with the person of Jesus Christ, and engaging in them for any other reason only creates extra baggage and unnecessary obstacles to our spiritual journey. The One who first invited me as a young boy to walk with him, was the only One who could now motivate me to journey on. In essence, the weight of the journey had caught up to me, and I needed to regain first love.

Debbie had been my first true love. It was on a warm August afternoon, my sophomore year of college, when I first saw her. My roommates suggested we go down to the ball field and watch a girls' intramural softball game. I certainly had no objection to *that* idea, so off we went. I was sitting in the bleachers watching the game, when the batter drilled a ground ball between short and third. The shortstop moved smoothly to her right, backhanded the grounder, planted her back foot, and rifled the ball from deep in the hole— effortlessly throwing the runner out at first. That was the first time I saw Debbie.

I saw her again later that evening. At the beginning of each school year, our college hosted a night of music for the incoming freshmen class. My roommates and I were bored, and since studying wasn't an option, we drifted over to the auditorium to check things out. I was surprised and delighted when the shortstop appeared on stage, her dusty softball uniform replaced with a yellow, chiffon gown, and proceeded to play a beautiful violin solo. I was smitten—an all-star athlete *and* a classical violinist. I was in love and the pursuit was on. We were married two years later, followed by twenty-five wonderful and fulfilling years together.

Three years after my wife's death, I saw her again.

In a dream, I was traveling with a friend on a rapid transit system through a major metropolitan city. The unusual thing about the particular tram we were riding was that as we stood in the middle aisle holding the safety bars overhead, a conveyor belt under our feet carried us forward. As can only happen in a dream, while the train moved down the tracks, simultaneously my friend and I, inside the train, were carried forward from car to car courtesy of the conveyor belt.

As I was being carried by the passengers seated on both sides of the train, I saw Debbie. Sitting alone, she was coming up on my right. She looked to be about twenty, the age she was when we first met. She wore a cool beret, cocked to one side, which covered her dark hair, except for a single braid which hung over her right front shoulder. Dressed in a mod brown tweed jacket, with a book bag and violin case at her side, she reminded me of a college student on her way to an audition. She was gorgeous. I was mesmerized. Our eyes met and she acknowledged me, but not as her husband, or even someone she knew, just as a fifty-year-old man traveling on the same train. I wanted to say something. Anything. "Debbie it's me! Don't you recognize me? Please come back to me!" I wanted to jump off the conveyor belt and talk to her, touch her. But I didn't; I couldn't; I froze. The ache in my heart intensified as the conveyor belt carried me all too quickly away from her. The dream ended and I awoke—yet all the feelings of first love remained.

Even the following morning as I recorded the dream in my journal, I felt my heart thawing and the warm feelings of first love lingered. As I further pondered on the dream throughout the day, it seemed to be foreshadowing a shift from my long winter season. I interpreted the dream as a message sent to tell me: *As you continue in the day-to-day activities of your life, you will unexpectedly encounter someone who will once again warm your heart and reawaken your love.* Five months later the dream came true. I'm now remarried and once again experiencing all the feelings of first love.

To a follower of Christ, times of difficulty, even though painful, can lead us back to our first love. These seasons of difficulty provide us with the opportunity to pause, remove the clutter, unload the excess baggage, and return to the true source of our life—the person of Jesus Christ. Like a wandering and weary traveler, the weight of my wife's passing forced me to do just that—to unload the baggage I could no longer carry—obligations and expectations, failures and regrets, broken promises and broken relationships—and return to a simple and pure devotion to the person of Jesus Christ.

Looking back, I now see God at work in me before, during, and after losing my first love. One of those events, which seemed to prepare me for what was about to come, occurred just before my wife's accident. I was teaching a series at the church I pastored, titled "Following Christ: More than a Nice Idea." In preparation for this sermon series, I had been rereading a Christian classic, *The Cost of Discipleship*, by Deitrich Bonhoeffer. Bonhoeffer was a pastor in Nazi Germany who refused to compromise with Hitler and the unethical government of his day and was ultimately executed for his stance.

A few days after my wife's funeral, I resumed my teaching series, and returned to reading Bonheoffer's book. The words on the pages were no longer just someone else's thoughts about following Christ, nor my teaching series just "another nice idea." They were both, now, very real and very relevant to my own journey in following Christ.

After more than forty years of following Christ, my wife's death challenged me to once again honestly grapple with the cost involved in following him.

Unfortunately, the Church in North America frequently presents an incomplete invitation to follow Christ. The offer is often, "Come to Christ and get everything fixed. Get your marriage fixed. Get your family fixed. Get your job fixed. Get your life fixed. Come to Jesus, get your sins forgiven, get eternal life, *and* get the American dream." Somehow, the cost involved in following Christ has been conveniently left out.

Dr. Larry Crabb makes this point uncomfortably clear when he writes, "The evangelical church has made a serious mistake. For years we've presented Christianity as little more than a means of escaping hell. Knowing Jesus has been reduced to a one-time decision that guarantees the chance to live in a perfect, pain-free world forever. Making our marriages work and our kids turn out well and our bank accounts comfortably bulge is not God's plan for our lives." [2]

A friend of mine frames this flawed invitation to follow Christ with these facetious words, "The invitation presented in the church to follow Jesus sounds like a country song being played backwards. *'Come to Jesus and get your wife back, your kids back, your house back, your truck back and even your dog back'*." This would be humorous if it weren't so grievous.

So that I am not misunderstood, let me make two points clear. First, the gospel unmistakably offers forgiveness of sins and secures our eternal destiny. Second, there *are* tangible benefits as a result of following Christ. These are both undeniable facts. I would suggest, however, that in our presentation of the gospel we have emphasized the front end— forgiveness of sins, and the back end—eternal life, but have almost completely avoided the cost involved in following Christ, sadly making it an incomplete and inaccurate representation of what it means to follow him.

Too much of what's pawned off as Christianity, particularly in the Western world, is partial at best, and some of it an outright perversion. How did we ever get the idea of a safe and costless Christianity from a radical movement whose central metaphor is a cross and whose leaders were executed? We have conveniently left out the call to follow Christ in spite of persecution or suffering, betrayal or abandonment, tragedy or loss, difficulties or disappointments. When following Christ doesn't turn out as marketed, many Christians, infected with this deficient understanding of the gospel, are left dazed and disillusioned. Others, believing they were sold a product that hasn't delivered as promised, sometimes outright abandon their commitment to Christ.

My wife's passing forced me to evaluate and then excavate portions of my own faulty foundations. I had to painstakingly deconstruct a commitment to follow Christ partially built upon comfort and convenience. I had to turn from a gospel diluted with materialism and consumerism, and convert to a gospel requiring costly discipleship.

As a way to revisit what it meant to fully follow Christ, I reacquainted myself with the lives of many earlier Christ followers. I revisited the life of the early church, observed as they repeatedly faced persecution and suffering, yet passionately journeyed on. I read the writings of men and women throughout the history of the church who paid a price to follow him, yet courageously continued on. Through the pages of the gospels, I revisited the life of Jesus, observed the price he paid, and freshly recommitted to his call to, "Come and follow me."

I know firsthand what it's like to experience first love and then lose it. Today, however, my relationship with Christ is as passionate as it was when I first fell in love with him at the age of seven. A recent journal entry reflects my current relationship with him.

I'm struck by the simplicity of Jesus' words to, "Come follow me." We often make following Christ way too complicated—programs, activities, events, theologies, obligations, formulas. If we are not careful, we can join with the religious leaders that Jesus charged in his day of piling burdens on top of already existing burdens.

Jesus has a way of getting us back to basics— back to life—when he invites us to come and follow him. In a world of noise, outside and inside the church, we need to heed his invitation, silence the confusion, cut through the clutter, and calm the complexity. I have found that true life isn't in the activity or the external, but it begins and is sustained from my journey with Him from within.

Revisiting these two foundations, God is God and I am not, and the cost involved in following Christ, provided me the secure footing from which I could safely journey on. In the next chapter, I will share with you *the* central lesson I've learned about navigating life.

So don't stop now. Let's journey on.

Reflection/Discussion Questions

1. Have you picked up any extra baggage over the years on your spiritual journey that are currently weighing you down? If so, what are they?

2. Are there any areas in your spiritual life where duty has replaced devotion, routine has replaced relationship, or activity has replaced adventure? If yes, where and what are they?

3. Are there obligations and expectations, failures and regret, broken promises or broken relationships that are weighing you down?

4. Do you need to return to your "first love?"

5. How does your interpretation of the difficulties you experience in your own life, reveal your understanding of following Christ? Have you bought into the front side of following him (salvation) and the back end (heaven and eternal life) but avoided or neglected the potential cost of following him?

6. Have you bought into a consumer driven Christianity? If so, how does this affect your response to the difficulties you've experienced along the way?

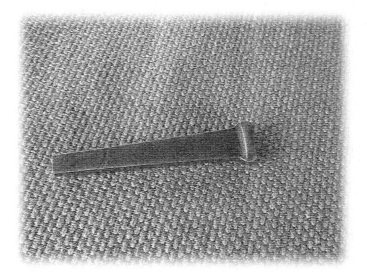

CHAPTER SEVEN

Shaped By Life

Now with God's help, I shall become myself.

- Søren Kierkegaard

Life shapes us.

Henry Ward Beecher wrote, "God ask no man whether he will accept life. That is not the choice. The only choice is how." [1] The unexpected turns we experience throughout our journey are significant and the impact incurred on our lives should not be trivialized. What's most important however, aren't necessarily the details of the difficulties, but our response to them. I believe how we respond to adversity is *the central lesson* we must learn in order to wisely navigate through life's unexpected turns.

Within weeks of my wife's accident, it became clear that how I responded to her death and the difficult days ahead would indeed shape me. It wasn't a question of *if* the tragedy would shape me, it was only a question of *how* it would shape me. Would it change me for the better or for the worse? Would it move me towards or away from who I hoped to become? The answer would be determined by my response. The choice was mine.

Earlier in my life, my approach during times of difficulty was never, "How should I respond?" In fact, my pattern was to react the exact opposite. I despised difficulties. I fainted during trials. I ran from setbacks. I avoided suffering. My basic response was to cry and complain, kick and scream, whine and pout throughout the entire ordeal. Pity parties were a regularly scheduled event.

Then ten years before my wife's accident, I experienced a fundamental shift in my approach toward times of difficulty. This shift began while reading the following Scripture: *"Consider it pure joy whenever you face trials of many kinds, because you know that the testing of your faith develops perseverance. Perseverance must finish its work so that you may be mature and complete."* [2]

Although I had read this particular passage on many occasions, this time it took hold of me in a different way. I began to understand and embrace it with deeper meaning. I realized that "difficulties will always be part of the journey— it's called 'life.' And, since adversity is unavoidable, I should at least grow from them as I go through them." This simple insight set in motion a profound change in my life. Looking back, I now recognize I was graciously being prepared for what was to come.

Over time, this new outlook radically reoriented my mental attitude toward difficulties, and dramatically re-wired my emotional response to them. Instead of viewing trials as simply unwanted pain, I now approached them as opportunities for personal growth. Instead of seeing adversity as nothing more than suffering and setback, I now embraced them as an occasion to be shaped into the person I wanted to become. In reality, this new approach reframed my worldview toward all of life.

Every one of us is being shaped in some fashion. As Dallas Willard, a notable writer on the subject explains, "Spiritual formation, (i.e., the process of being shaped) without regard to any specifically religious context or tradition, is the process by which the human spirit or will are given a definite 'form' or character. It is a process that happens to everyone. The most despicable as well as the most admirable of persons have had a spiritual formation. Terrorist as well as saints are the outcome of spiritual formation. Their spirits or hearts have been formed. Period." [3]

For a follower of Christ, the ultimate goal of our formation is to increasingly become like the One we are following. A particular Scripture describes the objective this way. *"God knew what he was doing from the beginning. He decided from the outset to shape the lives of those who love him along the same lines as the life of His son. The Son stands first in the line of humanity he restored. We see the original and intended shape of our lives there in him."* [4]

The Bible compares spiritual formation for followers of Christ to the development of the embryo in its mother's womb and the process of a caterpillar changing into a butterfly. [5] The Christian faith asserts that as we work with God and He works with us, transformation will take place; a frog can become a prince, an ugly duckling can become a swan, and a terrorist can become a saint.

God is so committed to this process of transformation—shaping us into the likeness of His son—that He will use *all things* toward that end. To be clear, I didn't say (nor do I believe) that God *causes every thing* that happens to us. For example, breaking the natural laws that govern our universe, such as standing in front of a moving locomotive, falling from a hundred foot cliff, or two cars colliding, bring their own consequences. Our own choices also bring consequences: abusing our bodies through alcohol or driveness, destroying relationships through bitterness or betrayal, experiencing financial calamity through greed or mismanagement—or through many other endless ways. And sadly, we are not immune from the consequences of the actions perpetrated on us by others—rape, abuse, assault, abandonment, fraud, unfaithfulness… I find it hard to blame God for these cause and effect consequences. But this chapter isn't about *why* bad things happen, but *how* we respond to what happens.

I never imagined God would *allow* such a tragedy to occur in my life. But I quickly realized that if I continued to trust Him in the process, He would use it, like a chisel in the hands of a gifted sculptor, to shape me. Once I understood that God's ultimate goal for my life wasn't happiness, success, prosperity, or personal satisfaction (although He was not opposed to such things), but rather spiritual transformation, I began to more willingly embrace difficulty as a tool to shape me into the person I hoped to become. Grasping this reality guided my response toward constructive changes and away from destructive ones.

For those who do not hold a Christian worldview, the reality that our response to life shapes us, still holds true. Over the years, I've observed a variety of ways people have responded to difficulty and as a result, have been shaped by it. Some become hardened, others more humble. Some become cynical, others more grateful. Some grow to resent life; others discover a deeper purpose to life. Some wilt, others bloom. Some learn to hate, others learn to love. Some become hopeless; others become resilient. Some are blown off course; others are moved toward their destiny.

Life shapes us. No one's exempt. It's not a question of *if*, only a question of *how*. Our response determines the outcome. The choice is ours!

I clearly remember the morning this principle, "How will I respond?" took root in my own life. A few days after my wife's passing I was making my bed, when right in the middle of tucking in the sheets, my anger surged. A voice in my head screamed, "I'm a forty-seven-year-old man, starting life all over, making my king-sized bed, alone. I hate this. This isn't fair!" As I straightened the sheets, arranged the comforter, and fluffed the pillows, the irrepressible thoughts continued and the anger intensified. Then, like a loose cog clicking into place, it became crystal clear, "How I respond, even in these moments of seemingly ordinary activities, will determine who I become." That simple thought was revolutionary. As I made my bed the following weeks, instead of occasions for anger and resentment, these domestic chores became opportunities to practice servanthood and humility, patience and peace, contentment and gratitude.

This new approach wasn't limited to making my bed but extended to shopping at the grocery store, washing dishes, paying the bills, and doing laundry. When the little old lady ahead of me in the express checkout line, chatted with the cashier about her latest doctor's visit, a recent trip to the casino, and updates on all twenty-nine grandchildren, would

I be pleasant and patient or rude and annoyed? After hitting the golf ball off the same tee into the same woods for the third time, would I be irate or graciously accept my golfing limitations? When the driver behind me honked within a nanosecond of the red light turning green, how would I respond? (I still have some work to do in this area.) All of my daily activities became sacred moments for meaningful formation.

As a way to *practice* positive responses in my daily activities, I began a very unusual ritual. Every morning as I got dressed, I picked up from my nightstand a small spike-like nail and put it into my pants pocket. The nail served as a tangible reminder of Christ's work on the cross and also a reminder to respond to everything that happened during my day in a way that moved me toward who I hoped to become. As I undressed in the evening, I returned the nail to my nightstand, ready to repeat the pattern the following morning. I performed this odd ritual each and every day for over a year.

So you don't think I'm *too* odd, I'm not suggesting living life as a masochistic monk. No one, at least in their right mind, should be out looking for difficulties—they seem to find us on their own. Nor should we gleefully welcome them when they do knock on our door. That *would* be odd. What I am suggesting is that the process of formation isn't as complicated nor as mysterious as we often make it. Our everyday routine provides endless opportunities to practice our responses in ways that shape us into the person we hope to become.

In his book *The Rhythm Of Life*, Mathew Kelley shares a story about the great violinist, Itzak Pearlman, which illustrates the importance of practice in the process of formation. Kelley writes,

> *At a charity reception Mr. Pearlman, stood in a roped off area greeting guests as they filed by. As one of the guest shook hands with the violinist he said, "Mr. Pearlman you were phenomenal tonight. Absolutely amazing." Pearlman smiled but said nothing. The man continued, "All my life I have had a great love of the violin, but I have never heard anyone play the violin as brilliantly as you did tonight." Pearlman smiled again, but said nothing, and the man continued, "You know Mr. Pearlman, I would give my whole life to be able to play the violin like you did tonight." Pearlman smiled again and said, "I have." [6]*

Similar to any accomplished artist or athlete, practice is necessary for transformation. Just imagine how many thousands of times a professional golfer has practiced hitting his seven iron. Because of his consistent practice, he is thoroughly prepared to accurately hit his seven iron as he approaches the eighteenth hole, one shot ahead, with millions of fans watching and millions of dollars on the line. Similarly, practicing our responses during the routine challenges of our daily activities sets in place the proper patterns and prepares us for the more difficult situations that are certain to come. It's not a matter of trying harder in the moment of challenge; it's a matter of training consistently leading up to the challenge.

To eliminate any confusion, practicing our responses isn't simply behavioral modification. For me, as a follower of Christ, it's a consistent decision of my will, agreeing with and aligning myself to my new nature (even though only in embryonic form), already brought about by my spiritual conversion. From the Christian perspective, this process of change occurs by the grace of God *and* in conjunction with our response.

Dallas Willard explains this symbiotic relationship between God's enablement and our effort with these words from Oswald Chambers, "The question of forming habits on the basis of the grace of God is a very vital one. If we refuse to practice, it is not God's grace that fails when a crisis comes, but our own nature. When the crisis comes, we ask God to help us, but He cannot if we have not made our nature our ally. The practicing is ours, not God's. God regenerates us—gives us a new life—and puts us in contact with all His divine resources, but He cannot make us walk according to His will." [7]

Becoming who we are meant to be, not only takes consistent practice, but it's also a lifelong process. The life of Abraham illustrates this point. The Bible says, "Abraham *became* the father of faith." This statement implies that his transformation, who he eventually became, didn't happen overnight. For Abraham the process took a hundred years! In obedience to God's direction, Abraham left his home of familiarity and along the journey faced many challenges: a business dispute with his nephew, the abduction and rescue of his wife, a successful battle against five kings, survival of a severe famine, ongoing marital problems, the rescue of

Lot from Sodom and Gomorrah, and then waiting thirty-two years for a promised son to be born. All of this occurred while traveling through foreign lands to an unknown destination.

Abraham *became* the father of faith, not in spite of these experiences along the way, but *because* of them. Even Abraham's defining act of faith—his willingness to sacrifice his son at God's request—did not transpire at the beginning of his journey, but at the end. His response to all the prior events in his journey prepared him for this single climatic challenge of faith. Abraham *became* the father of faith over a process experienced throughout the entirety of his life's journey.

It's important to recognize that the process of change doesn't occur in just one season or through one event. It's a process through the entirety of our journey that ultimately shapes us. This long-term and process-oriented perspective helps us embrace *all* the events in our life, not as separate or isolated incidents, but as interrelated and purposeful to our overall journey and ultimate destiny.

Several years have passed since I first practiced my odd ritual of carrying that spike-like nail in my pocket every day. Today that very same nail still sits on my nightstand and, just as a reminder, occasionally, I pick it up and carry it in my pocket for the day. In case you are wondering, no, I haven't obtained perfection nor has anyone submitted my name for sainthood. I am however, still being shaped by life and gratefully I can say, I'm gradually moving toward the person I hope to become.

Life will shape us. The choice is ours. Our response determines the outcome.

Who are you becoming? Who will you become?

Reflection/Discussion Questions

1. How have the unexpected turns in your life, shaped you?

2. Do you currently embrace difficulties as having a redemptive purpose in your life or do you run, kick, and scream throughout the process?

3. How is life currently shaping you? Are you becoming the person God designed and desires you to be?

4. Are you allowing the unforeseen turns in your life as tools to shape you more into the image of the Son?

5. Do you agree that God does not cause all things?

6. Do you agree that much of the tragedy we experience is either the result of:

   a) Breaking the natural laws that govern our universe

   b) The result of our own choices

   c) The result of the actions others perpetrated on us

7. Are you allowing the routine and everyday events of your life to shape you into who you want to become or away from it?

CHAPTER EIGHT

Fight for Life

The universe is at war.

- C.S. Lewis

I've never been much of a fighter. It's not part of my personality. I'm more of a dreamer. I prefer movies like *Peter Pan* and *Sleepless in Seattle* to *Braveheart*, *Gladiator*, or *Rocky*. And although I was physically bigger than most of my classmates, I still avoided fights.

But when I was a junior in high school, I did have a fight. The mayhem occurred in Miss Childress's fourth period history class. As we sat at our desks waiting for class to begin, a known bully began picking a fight with one of my friends—a well-liked, chubby, boyish, good-natured guy. Unprovoked, the bully reached under Bobby's desk, grabbed him by the feet and flipped him over backwards, desk and all. I looked at Bobby lying on the floor, his desk securely saddled around his generous waist, with panic on his face, and realized Bobby wasn't a fighter either. But, for that moment, on that day, I decided I would be. I went after the bully.

Initially, it was just a lot of male bravado. First with words, telling each other exactly what we were about to do to the other. I was honestly hoping it wouldn't go beyond this brief exchange of testosterone-loaded threats. But, with our classmates encircling us and cheering us on, like two prizefighters, the bully and I were quickly engaged in a full-fledged brawl.

Miss Childress arrived on the scene prepared to lecture on the War of 1812. Instead she found her class huddled around what looked like a WWF match. Frantically, she tried to break us up, but as the bully and I ricocheted from wall to wall, over desks, to the floor, and back around again, she ran from the room screaming for help.

It took a few teachers to end the fight. Our high school principal, Mr. Robinson, telephoned my dad, an admired and respected pastor in our small community, and then the battle really began. Dad took care of things rather swiftly and judiciously—can you say, "whoopin?" And that was the end of my fighting days.

Many years have passed since my eleventh-grade brawl, but the subsequent years have convinced me, more than ever, that I'm still in a fight. It's not a schoolyard scrap with an immature high school bully, it's a fight with an experienced opponent; one who's been fighting since the beginning of time. He's deliberate, determined, and can even be deadly.

C.S. Lewis clearly recognized the fight we are in when he wrote, "One of the things that surprised me when I first read the New Testament seriously was that it talked so much about a Dark Power in the universe—a mighty evil spirit who was held to be the Power behind death and disease and sin. The difference is that Christianity thinks this Dark Power was created by God, and was good when he was created, and went wrong. Christianity agrees… this universe is at war." [1]

Many people simply deny the existence of an evil being, relegating him to nothing more than a mythical or animated character sporting a red cape, horns, pitchfork, and tail. Others accept the possibility of his existence, yet downplay the notion of his direct involvement in their lives. Unfortunately, both ideas are misinformed. Denying his existence or down playing his involvement is to our detriment. Similar to an intruder prowling throughout our house as we sleep, leaving our enemy undetected allows him unlimited access and opportunity for harm. Don't misunderstand; I'm not proposing that Satan is the sole source behind every mishap in life, which would also be an overstated and inaccurate view. But I am contending, as C.S. Lewis recognized, we do have an enemy, and we are at war.

Another Christian scholar, R.C. Sproul, further explains the balance needed in assessing our enemy when he writes, "The pendulum of popular belief about Satan tends to swing between two extremes. On one side there are those who believe he doesn't exist at all, or if he does exist, he is a mere impersonal evil 'force,' sort of a collective evil that finds its origin in the sin of society. On the other side there are those who have a preoccupied fixation, a cultic focus of attention upon him that diverts their gaze from Christ. With either extreme, Satan gains some ground." [2]

It only takes a quick walk through the Bible to be thoroughly convinced that our journey runs directly through a battle zone. In the beginning, God created a perfect world. Satan countered, instigated a coup, and spoiled God's original paradise. Casualties followed: conflict, division, separation, banishment, and ultimately, death. Adam and Eve's perfect world was shattered, and paradise was lost.

Years later, God's chosen people fought to escape a life of bondage and find a life of freedom. A major battle ensued between God's representative Moses and Pharaoh, the king of Egypt. The outcome would determine slavery or liberty. Eventually, the children of Israel won the battle, but their fight had just begun. Their flight from captivity to freedom was marked with constant struggle. In fact, Israel's journey to reach their "promised land," and then once there, to keep it, could be summed up as one long, continuous battle.

Jesus further confirms the war we are in when he exposes Satan's single mission with these succinct words, "He comes *only* to kill, steal and destroy." [3]

The New Testament presents additional evidence of an enemy. One writer warns of Satan's schemes and then passionately instructs us to properly prepare for the fight. Still another New Testament writer compares our enemy to a lion always on the prowl, waiting for the opportune time to pounce on unsuspecting victims. Even the last book of the Bible, "Revelation," is full of imagery, stories, and language describing clashes of kingdoms, battles between good and evil, plots of revenge, and plans of one last epic battle.

From a Christian perspective, the evidence makes it clear that we are in a war. But even if you don't agree with the evidence found throughout the Bible, nor agree with the Christian worldview, don't our own struggles in life, as well as the evil acts committed through thousands of years of history, give credible cause to consider that we may have an enemy? Isn't it possible that at least *some* of what we experience in our daily battles are more than coincidence? Isn't it possible that Satan might exist and might be active in our world?

As difficult as life is, and as much evil as we see in our world, isn't it hard *not* to believe an enemy is somehow involved instigating and orchestrating at least some of the struggle? It seems to me there *must* be something *in addition* to our own fractured human condition and our broken social structures (although both certainly contribute to our struggle) to fully explain the evil witnessed in our world. It seems to me that any honest reflection on these examples would lead a reasonable person to at least consider that an enemy might exist and that we might somehow be involved in a war.

My own Christian belief, as well as my life experiences, and my observation of the lives of many others, has provided more than enough evidence to convince me that we do have an enemy and we are at war. Whatever your preference or personality is toward fighting, I would graciously suggest there *is* a fight going on and frankly, to refuse to acknowledge it, is to your own peril.

Over the years, I've observed (and experienced) a certain disturbing pattern in this fight for life. The pattern seems to be that a spiritual battle often occurs *before* spiritual advancement and then a spiritual battle often ensues *because* of the advancement.

All signs indicated that Debbie and I had just experienced some significant spiritual advancements. For twenty-two long years, the church I led met in a public high school auditorium. Early every Sunday morning, like clockwork, a committed crew began the process of setting up sound equipment, a welcome center, children's classrooms, resource and refreshment tables—everything needed to service a large, mobile church. Then, immediately after our Sunday service the crew tore it all down, loaded it back into a large truck and got ready to repeat this grinding work the following week. For the last fourteen of those twenty-two years, our dedicated congregation diligently worked to secure a permanent facility. Yet time after time and year after year we experienced roadblocks, setbacks, and delays.

After all the years of striving and struggling, our church family finally secured land, built a facility, and obtained our dream of a permanent "church home." Once in our new building, we experienced steady growth, grew deeper as a spiritual community, and witnessed many authentic spiritual seekers exploring the claims of Christ and crossing the line into genuine believing faith. It was obvious to all that our church family was experiencing some long-awaited and long-fought-for breakthroughs, and my wife Debbie was front and center in this entire advancement.

Then nine months after we moved into our new church facility,

Debbie's accident and death.

Along with our congregation's advancement, we had also experienced significant forward progress within the larger Christian community in our city and the surrounding region. For more than fifteen years, Debbie and I had been working with other Christian leaders to see transformation occur in our area. These relationships represented a broad cross section of church denominations and affiliations, suburban and urban congregations, and various ethnic expressions. Because of this growing trust among area pastors and churches, a vision for partnerships within the Christian community in our region continued to emerge and together we were beginning to make an impact.

Then, my wife's accident and death.

Prayer efforts in our city had also made significant advancements. I had personally been involved in leading a large network of over 600 people, who prayed specifically for spiritual advancement in our region. In addition to this large prayer network, I was also directly involved in helping launch another prayer ministry whose focus was to pray, twenty-four hours a day, seven days a week, for spiritual advancement in our city and the surrounding region.

Then, my wife's accident and death.

How should I interpret my wife's death in the light of these advancements? Was her death a result of the battle for life? Was she a causality of war? Or was this all just coincidental?

As I struggled with these disturbing questions, I remembered two separate incidents that had occurred prior to Debbie's accident, which gave me further cause for alarm and concern.

Approximately six months before her death, Debbie arrived home from work one afternoon visibly shaken. I asked her why she was so upset and she immediately blurted out, "Kenny, I was almost killed today." She then related to me the details of the near fatal mishap. Walking from the mall, she was crossing the parking lot on the way to her car, when a man backing out of his parking spot recklessly gunned his car backwards, just as Debbie was walking behind it, missing her by inches.

I don't recall my wife ever being this shook up over such a situation. The alarm and uneasiness caused by this incident, like a stalker hidden in the shadows, followed her for more than a week. It seems to me now that this incident was not just a minor mishap in a mall parking lot, but rather something deeper, something more sinister was at work.

The second incident that occurred, which was even more disturbing than the first, was a dream I had had several months before my wife's death. In the dream, Debbie and I, along with the leadership team from the church that I pastored, had been dropped behind enemy lines. My sense was that we were in an eastern bloc country of the former Soviet Union. As a group, we secretly gathered in a small, dimly-lit living room. Debbie and I were sitting on a couch with a window directly behind us, the rest of the team closely huddled around. As we discussed our covert plans, a shadowy figure appeared in the window behind us and shot my wife in the back of the head. As she slumped lifeless to the floor, the team scattered in different directions. I awoke from the dream. I'm very cautious about "reading too much into our dreams," but all I can say is that within a year of the dream, Debbie *was* dead and within three years, all of the team members present in the dream *had* disbanded and scattered.

Were these two incidents just coincidence?

Since I had already settled my belief that God is in control of all things, as well as embraced the fact that He will use all things in the process of my transformation, I now had to consider the disturbing question regarding what role, if any, did the spiritual battle play in my wife's death? The question of Satan's role in the pre-established plans of God and the destructive activities of an enemy in a world controlled by God are difficult questions and ones long debated in theological and philosophical circles. And quite honestly, diving into this question makes some people very uncomfortable. Since I had been schooled in theology, I was familiar with the various answers offered to this complex question. But with my wife's passing, this question was no longer just some academic discussion but now, for me, a very personal pursuit. I was compelled to re-explore this question, consciously aware that the conclusions I came to, I could not conveniently avoid. So I began to ask the hard questions.

What is God's part? If God knew Debbie's accident was going to happen why didn't he prevent it? Why didn't God warn us? Or did He? Why didn't God delay her leaving the house that day, saving us from the entire tragedy? Did God not know that the accident was going to occur, and Satan had simply won a blow in the battle? Or did God know it and allowed it anyway? If so, why? What sense does that make?

What is man's part? Are we caught in a cosmic battle between God and Satan in which the winner is determined by what we, as humans, do or don't do? If we did more warring against our enemy, would our efforts prevent some of the enemy's attacks and subsequent tragedies and loss? What was my responsibility in this tragedy? Would it have made a difference if I had prayed more? Should I have been more discerning the morning before my wife left the house? Did God attempt to warn me of Satan's ambush, but I was just too busy to hear and heed the warning?

And finally, what is Satan's part? Is every difficulty or devastation the result of the devil? Is any of it? Is none of it? What latitude does Satan possess apart from God's permission? Is Satan simply a pawn in God's plans, with his acts of evil ultimately only serving God's final agenda?

Even as I write this, I'm still not certain of all the answers to these difficult questions, but my search has led me to at least one firm conclusion.

I'm convinced more than ever, that we are in a spiritual battle. My own experience has convinced me that God is good, in control, and involved in every detail of my life. While at the same time, I'm just as convinced that I have a real enemy who hates me and wants to destroy any and everything in my life that he can. I fully agree with John Eldredge when he describes our battle for life with these sobering words:

> By all means, God intends life for us. But right now that life is *opposed*. It doesn't just roll in on a tray. There is a thief. He comes to kill, and steal,

and destroy. In other words, yes, the offer is life, but you're going to have to fight for it because there's an Enemy in your life with a different agenda. There *is* something set against us. We are at war. [4]

I've come to the place in my journey where I now willingly embrace these two seemingly contradictory truths—that God is good and in control but that we have an enemy who battles against us—and now that I'm convinced of this spiritual battle, I'm more fully engaged in it.

When I was eight, Billy Stanfield, a kid from my neighborhood, would regularly call me and invite me over to box. With my heart pounding, I would slam down the phone, race across the open field next to my house, dart across a busy two-lane road, jump a ditch, and land in his back yard. Billy would be there waiting for me with a pair of boxing gloves tucked under his arms. Nestled between two oak trees along the fence row in Billy's back yard, was our boxing arena—an 8 foot by 8 foot woodshed, with a broken off door, no windows, and a dirt floor. Once inside, like two miniature gladiators, we would lace up our gloves and prepare for battle.

Billy's reason for boxing was a bit twisted. He was smaller than most kids his age and what he lacked in size he was determined to make up with toughness and tenacity. Since I was bigger than most kids my age, I became Billy's chosen one to help him overcome his insecurities about his size. A sick reason to fight I know, but like a good friend and neighbor should, I graciously obliged.

Even before our fight started, we both knew how it would end—I would win. I always did. Thus, we had a pre-battle agreement: when Billy got so dazed that he either didn't know where he was, could no longer get up from the dirt floor, or simply said, "Enough beating for now," we would unlace the gloves, head toward the house (with Billy stumbling toward it), and like good fighting friends should, end the day with a cool glass of lemonade.

My boxing bouts with Billy remind me of our own battle with the enemy. We get knocked around so frequently, the blows coming from so many different directions, that we are often left dazed. But what's so alarming to me isn't the dizziness or damage left from the pounding, but our lack of awareness that we are even in a fight. All of this discussion about fighting an enemy isn't to leave us weary and wary, but rather a reminder for us to be aware. Being convinced we are at war is half the battle, being diligently engaged in it is the crucial other half.

Over a century ago, one Christian leader, Watchmen Nee, suggested that one of Satan's tactics is to simply wear us down with the daily battles of everyday life. I agree. Like any soldier engaged in war, over time, battle fatigue sets in. It takes deep root in our soul, wearing us down and causing some of us to simply endure life, hoping life will take us where we want to go. And for others the weariness from war causes us to hunker down and simply try to protect any advancement already gained.

Realizing spiritual advancement is costly, I totally understand why some Christian leaders decide, whether consciously or unconsciously, to no longer aggressively forge ahead in life or ministry. I likewise understand why many Christians, weary from the battle, stop fighting and start drifting, and like a raft on an open sea let life take them wherever it wants.

After some honest reflection, I had to admit to myself that during the years prior to my wife's passing, I hadn't been as fully aware of, or as vigilant towards the enemy and his schemes as I needed to be. Life had worn me down. Battle fatigue had settled in. And like Billy, the battle had left me dazed.

I'm no longer a testosterone-charged teenager fighting with a schoolyard bully protecting my buddy Bobby, but I'm aware, now more than ever, that this journey called life is a battle and whatever our personality or preference is toward fighting, we are in a war and we must fight for life. I am. I hope you are, too.

Reflection/Discussion Questions

1. Do you believe we have an enemy? If yes, why (on what evidence)? If not, why (on what evidence)?

2. Describe a time when you felt you were in a spiritual battle?

3. Do you agree that spiritual backlash usually occurs as a result of spiritual advancements?

4. On which side of the pendulum do you lean? That Satan doesn't exist, or if he does, he is merely an impersonal evil force? Or do you have a preoccupied fixation upon him?

5. Do you think Satan was (is) involved in any of the unforeseen turns in your life?

6. Are you awake and aware to Satan's potential activities in your situation?

CHAPTER NINE

Looking Up

He died at thirty, they buried him at sixty.

- Mark Twain

A few months after my wife's death, a young man who had experienced a tragedy similar to my own, came to visit me. Prior to Mike's visit, a mutual friend filled me in on the details of his situation. To celebrate their one-year wedding anniversary, Mike and his wife had planned a special weekend away. Needing to earn some extra money for their trip, he had worked a double shift and arrived home, picked up his wife, and they headed out for their time away. As exhaustion overcame excitement, Mike fell asleep at the wheel and slammed into the rear of a semi-truck, killing his wife and unborn child.

He now sat across the table from me at a local diner. What do you say? We ate lunch, took a long walk in the park, and finally sat down on a large boulder overlooking a lake. At first our conversation was awkward, but eventually it turned to the details of the accident and the devastation left in its wake. He talked about his pain, his confusion, and his deep feelings of regret and guilt. I asked him about the state of his soul, his fractured faith, and his uncertain future.

After a few hours, I gently offered him some advice out of my own experience and brokenness. "Mike, one of the things I'm learning in the midst of my own confusion and pain is the importance of keeping my dreams alive." As soon as I said it, I could see in his eyes just how absurd these words seemed to him. He didn't say it, that would be impolite, but I knew what he was thinking, "Keep my dreams alive at a time like this? You've got to be kidding!"

A saying I coined several years ago, I find to be even truer today. *Dreams disconnected from reality lead to delusion, but the demanding realities of life disconnected from dreams lead to despair.* Dreams provide hope, and hope is *essential* for life. Whether we fulfill all of our dreams or only a portion of them, in some ways is secondary. Having dreams and keeping them alive while navigating through life is what's important and even essential, for our very survival.

Charles Swindoll uses these poetic words to further describe our basic need for hope. "Take from a man his wealth, and you hinder him; take from him his purpose, and you slow him down. But take from man his hope, and you stop him. He can go on without wealth, and even without purpose, for a while. But he will not go on without hope." [1]

Numerous studies substantiate this point. One such study, reported in an article in *New Yorker Magazine*, researched the mortality rate of 4,500 widowers. The findings showed that within six months of their wives' deaths, the widowers' mortality rate was 40 percent higher than other married men of the same age. [2] Other studies concerning Holocaust survivors and P.O.W.s present the same evidence. [3] Hope is essential for survival.

Even Dante, in his classic work, *The Divine Comedy*, understood the necessity of hope. With great insight, he wrote the inscription over the entrance to hell to read, "All hope abandon, Ye who enter here."[4]

David Jacobsen experienced hell but didn't abandon hope. As a P.O.W. in a Beirut cell he was routinely tortured for over seventeen months. When he was finally released and returned home a newspaper reporter asked him, "Mr. Jacobsen, what kept you alive during the many months of extreme cruelty and the daily uncertainty of whether you would live or die?" His immediate response, "Hope was the nourishment for my survival." [5]

It isn't only during times of tragedy, like Mike's or my own, when dreams need to be kept alive, but dreams also need to be kept alive throughout the daily demands and drudging routine of life.

Although I held many jobs in my youth, the hardest job I ever had was the summer I was sixteen. I was a "mud man" for a local brick-laying crew. My job was to keep mortar, bricks, and scaffolding supplied for three veteran bricklayers. I began each day making mortar, mixing just the right combination of sand, water, and dye. Then I dumped the mortar into a wheelbarrow, and like an Indy 500 driver, steered at breakneck speeds around scattered debris, dutifully delivering my cargo. Next, I hurried to a pallet and loaded sixteen bricks, eight bricks in each tong, one tong in each hand. I stumbled over scrap wood and broken bricks, quickly unloading more needed cargo. I chugged down some cool water, wiped the sweat from my face and scurried off to tear down scaffolding used in the last section of the wall and then quickly set it up wherever it was needed—further up the wall, down the wall, or around the corner to the next wall. While dancing with each dangling section of scaffolding, I anxiously awaited the shout from an impatient bricklayer, "Hey, I need more bricks and mortar!"

This crazy pace continued all day. Making mortar, carrying bricks, moving scaffolding, mortar, bricks, scaffolding, mortar, bricks, scaffolding... (I think I understand how the Children of Israel felt in Egypt.) Not only did I do this grueling work *all day* but I did it all day *every day* for the entire summer.

Although you're probably not a "mud man," the routine of your life may be a grind just the same. Like a sunburn on a cloudy day, the pace of life can catch us unaware. We get up in the morning facing another day of duties and deadlines, run off to work (usually already late), stop to pick up a cup of coffee, fight through traffic, and hurry into the office— where all the demands of the day persistently await us.

During one season of my life, I stumbled into such a rut. Leaving my house at the exact same time every morning, I dropped my son off at school, stopped by the same donut shop and ordered the same nutritious breakfast, "Could I have a small coffee, with double cream, double sugar, and one raisin bran muffin, please?" Then I sputtered on down the same road, to the same office complex, sat in the same chair, behind the same desk, doing the same tasks. Like any well-trained circus animal, my monotonous and mindless pattern continued for months.

Everyone's routine differs to some degree, yet all of our routines can be numbing just the same. You make breakfast, get the kids off to school, clean the kitchen, make the beds, pay the bills, answer the phone, do laundry, plan supper, go grocery shopping, pick the kids up, go to soccer practice, (or dance practice, or karate class, or Brownies, or Boy Scouts or piano lessons or ...), help with homework, referee a sibling spat, cook supper, wash the dishes, help with some more homework, referee another sibling spat, set the alarm and stumble into bed—numbingly aware that the same grind awaits you the next day and the next and the next.

These scenarios may or may not describe your daily routine, but unfortunately, for far too many of us our pace of life is still very similar to the grind of a "mud man."

The danger of the dailyness of life is that it can, and often does, destroy the very *heart* of life. The accumulation of situation after situation reduces us to mere zombies. We stumble through life keeping the body parts moving, but our hearts are barely alive. We're breathing, but not really living. Life has beaten us up, thrown us down, and robbed us of our dreams. Sure, we are still sucking in air, still taking up space on the planet, but are we really living?

Mark Twain summed up this kind of life when he remarked about the death of an acquaintance with these witty words, "He died at thirty; they buried him at sixty." [6]

My son is a musician. He writes, records, produces, and plays music. It's his passion. For his birthday, his wife, Amanda, surprised him with tickets to a Bob Dylan concert. Like many musicians, Britton listens to Dylan's music, studies his lyrics, reads biographies about him, and watches documentaries on the folk-rock legend. But Britton never had the opportunity to attend a live Dylan concert. A few days after the concert I asked him what he thought of Dylan. His response was interesting and insightful: He said, "Dad, Dylan sure looks old and worn out from all the years on the road, but when he plays, *he still has passion."* I immediately thought of the line by William Wallace in the movie *Braveheart*, "We know that all men die, but not all men live." [7]

Dreams and passion are intricately connected. Both are essential for fully living life: We can *exist* without them, but can we *live* without them?

Bruce Wilkinson, in his book *The Dream Giver*, makes this connection between dreams and passion clear with these words,

> No matter where I travel in the world—whether among hard-charging Manhattan urbanites or villagers in southern Africa—I have yet to find a person who didn't have a dream. They may not be able to describe it. They may have forgotten it. They may no longer believe in it.
>
> But it's there.
>
> Like the genetic code that describes your unique passion and abilities, your Big Dream has been woven into your being from birth. You're the only person with a Dream quite like yours. And you have it for a reason: *to draw you toward the kind of life you were born to love!* [8]   *[emphasis added]*

In the heart of every person lives a dream. We may have to silence some internal voices of self-doubt or remove layers of expectations imposed on us by others, but if we listen close enough, or drill deep enough, we'll find a dream—it's there, pulsating faintly, but still alive. Every one of us has it—a longing for more, a passion that wants to surface, a dream that wants to survive.

It's unfortunate, but some find all this encouragement about keeping dreams alive and pursuing our passions as nothing more than idealistic romanticism or impractical sentimentalism. Still others view it as just another creative way to veil increased selfishness. I'm certainly not suggesting more materialistic, hedonistic, or narcissistic pursuits. Evaluating our motives for pursuing certain dreams is important. But what I am suggesting is that it is narrow and arrogant to catalog the dreams of others into ones that are worldly and ones that are holy, ones that are altruistic and ones that are selfish, ones that are secular and ones that are sacred. Some, in an attempt to play God, dissect the motives of others, and sadly, as a result, cause some people's passion to be squelched and their dreams to be shelved. Fortunately for us, God is the dream giver and in the end, only His vote counts.

Currently, as a follower of Christ who's passionately pursuing some of my own dreams, I agree with Erwin McManus's perspective when he writes, "When you make God your primary passion, He transforms all the passions of your heart. The result of this transformation is that it will be God's pleasure to fulfill those passions. …your passions become your best compass for your spiritual journey. When

God is your desire, you can trust the passions of your heart. It is in this state that you can most fully live a uniquely passionate life." [9]

I'm still inspired by the line in the movie, *Chariots of Fire,* when Eric Liddell tells his sister, "Jenny when I run, I feel His pleasure." [10]

Whether your dream is to become a published author, run the Boston marathon, perform at Carnegie Hall, run a Fortune 500 company, build orphanages around the world, stamp out world hunger, or be the world's best stay at home mom—if it's a passion from God and you're doing it with a passion to please God, then pursue it. And may it give you immeasurable pleasure!

In the months (and years) following my wife's passing, like Eric Liddell, I too had to honestly assess what brought me pleasure. After being in a healthy and fulfilling marriage for over twenty-five years, and then living as a widower for almost four years, my purposeful identification and passionate pursuit of proper pleasures kept my soul safe and sane during that lonely season of my life.

What I discovered during that time in my life was that our soul, that inner part of us, is created to be fed. There are both proper and improper ways to nurture our soul. But one way or another, it will be fed. I believe one of the reasons many good people get trapped in harmful pleasures—gambling, pornography, illicit relationships, excessive entertainment, over eating or whatever drug of choice it is—is because they often haven't identified the appropriate activities that feed their soul. Then, when times of disappointment, seasons of intense demands, or periods of prolonged difficulties occur, and as a result of the soul's need for nourishment only increases, the allurement to inappropriate activities intensifies. I understand this temptation. I identify with these allurements.

C.S. Lewis also understood these allurements. In his book, *The Screwtape Letters*, Lewis gives great insight for the need to engage in proper pleasure and as a result deter harmful ones. In one scene, Uncle Screwtape is chiding his demon protégé, Wormwood, because he's allowed his "patient" (the person he's been assigned to win over to evil) to read a book he *really enjoyed* and take a walk in the country that *filled him with joy*. Screwtape scorns Wormwood with these words, "In other words you allowed him two *real positive pleasures*. Were you so ignorant as not to see the danger of this? The man who truly and disinterestedly enjoys any one thing in the world for its own sake, and without caring two pence what other people say about it, is by that very fact forewarned against some of our subtlest modes of attack." [11] [emphasis added] In short, what Lewis is pointing out in this exchange between Screwtape and Wormwood is that participating in proper pleasure reduces the allurement of improper ones.

Another Christian thinker, John Piper, explains the same idea this way: "Sin is what we do when our hearts are not satisfied with God," [and I would add] "nor satisfied with the pleasures He provides." [12] Certainly, this emphasis on pleasure will seem far too hedonistic to some. But isn't it true that we dishonor God as much by fearing and avoiding pleasure as we do by our dependence upon it or only living for it? The Christian message isn't the elimination of desire, but the transformation of it.

My own experience with pleasure is that a hurried and barren soul is a weak and susceptible one. And unfortunately, our culture isn't an ally with us in this battle. Our often driven and fast pace lives seldom leave room for the simple pleasures, and as a result only add to the power of unhealthy allurements. A starving soul will not be ignored forever. We must stop the insane pace of life long enough to identify and enjoy the proper pleasures that feed our soul.

For me, ways to nurture my soul are found in simple things—a meaningful conversation, time with friends, a long walk in the park, an enjoyable meal, a summer's sunset, a walk along the beach, a good book. My soul is well fed when I take time to think deeply, make space for silence and solitude, take time to create, or slow down and explore the beauty of nature.

What feeds my soul may or may not be what feeds yours. Certainly the configuration and complexity of every soul is different. But the question still needs to be asked: In the midst of the demands of life, have you identified the appropriate pleasures that nourish your soul and are you deliberately setting aside time and creating routines to feed your soul?

Almost a year to the exact day of my wife's passing a close friend invited me to lunch. As we ended our meal, he handed me a package and asked me to open it. The gift was a photograph he had taken and framed, intentionally waiting until this occasion to present it to me. As I unwrapped and viewed the photo it was as if I was standing on the near side of a large lake looking toward the horizon. The sun is rising, and a tangerine orange hue is reflecting off the water, which in turn is coloring the underside of the clouds as they pass overhead and away. Sun light replaces darkness, apricot clouds replace black ones. What I found magical about the photo was how it focuses on the horizon, and by looking toward the horizon was the only perspective which reveals the glory of the photo.

He didn't say anything. He didn't need to. I easily grasped its meaning. In the midst of difficult times, keep looking at the horizon. The sun will rise, the clouds will pass.

After three-and-a-half years as a widower, I met someone extraordinary, fell in love, and got engaged. My son Britton, who had watched me go through this lonely season of my life, wrote and performed a song for me at my wedding reception. He appropriately called it, *Father, Don't Give Up.* Some of the words are:

If your life was written like a story
Only half the book is read
And though the middle holds for us no glory
The best part is for the end

Don't say goodbye, but say hello
If you never try, then you'll never know
And if the days go on, then so can you
Father, don't give up too soon.

In the silence, when the darkness seeks you
Always keep this thought in mind
The morning is coming, promising to greet you
To remind you you're alive

Don't say goodbye, but say hello
If you never try, then you'll never know
And if the storms move on, then so can you
Father, don't give up too soon.

At the age of twenty-four, after graduating from college, I moved to Regina, Saskatchewan, a city on the Canadian prairie. The terrain was bare, the winters brutal. Growing up in the rolling hills and wooded countryside of west Tennessee was entirely different from my new home on the wide-open, wintry plains of Canada. Shortly after I arrived, a tough and weathered Norwegian farmer took it upon himself to give the new southern kid in town some important Canadian prairie wisdom (although I don't really remember asking for any). With his gruff voice, well-leathered face and steely blue eyes staring at me, he said, "If you ever get caught in a Saskatchewan snowstorm, if at all possible, find shelter, and stay put until the storm passes." (I didn't think that was rocket-science advice, but I nodded in agreement nonetheless.) With his wisdom continuing to roll off his tongue he added, "But if you ever have to walk out of a blizzard, first find a visual marker, any kind—a large tree, a red barn, a porch light, a tree line—and once you start walking keep your eyes fixed on that marker and no matter what, keep walking in that direction." Then poking his crooked index finger just inches from my face, he drove his point home: "Because son, most people who get lost and die in a prairie snowstorm do so by walking around in circles with their heads down. So keep your head up, fix your eyes on the marker, and steadily move forward."

Writing *Unexpected* is the result of me looking up and keeping my dreams alive. I first had the desire to write when I was in college, and now after all of these years, having my first book written and published is the fulfillment of that dream. And although I never imagined that my wife's passing would be the reason for writing my first book, the process of writing *Unexpected* has provided me hope in the midst of pain, clarity in the midst of confusion, and expectation in the midst of uncertainty. Yes, dreams *do* provide hope, and hope *does* nourish our soul and both are needed so we can passionately journey on.

I'm not sure where Mike's journey has taken him over the last several years, but I hope he's dreaming, and looking up toward the horizon. And I hope the same is true of you. Keep your dreams alive! Feed your soul! Live life! It's the only one we get and now is the only chance we get to live it.

Come along with me as I tell you about a real dream—one that I'll never forget!

Reflection/Discussion Questions

1. Are you still pursuing any dreams? If so, what are they and how are you pursuing them. If not, why?

2. Are you still living or are you just waiting to be buried?

3. Do you know what proper activities feed your soul? If so, what are they?

4. Is there a dream still alive in your heart, but for the time being you've covered it up? If so, what is it and are you willing to once again uncover it?

5. What brings you pleasure?

6. In the midst of your pain or confusion, are you still "looking up?"

10 · 18 · 1956

DEBBIE ROBERTS

3 · 12 · 2004

CHAPTER TEN

Preparing for Death

Death is the end to every person; the living should take it to heart.

- Solomon

When my wife was pronounced dead on that Friday afternoon, March 12th, 2004, a long time friend standing next to me said, "Kenny, you can't prepare for things like this in a day."

There in the hospital room with my wife's body lying in front of me, I realized the truth of my friend's simple but insightful comment. The choices I had made and the patterns I had established up to that irreversible moment would now set the course for the rest of my life. I recognized the same would also be true for my two adult children. The values and principles their mother and I had instilled in them would likewise set the course for the rest of their lives.

It's true for all of us. How we live today prepares us (or doesn't prepare us), for tomorrow.

I've always loved the fact that Jesus was a realist. He wasn't, as some movie makers have painted him, a pie in the sky, glazed over, starry-eyed messianic mystic. He was a realist who warned us that life wouldn't always be kind or fair and that difficulties would be a normal part of the human experience. But Jesus didn't just leave us with these words warning us of difficult days, instead he graciously gave us clear instructions on how to prepare *today* for difficult days which are certain to come.

Jesus explained the importance of preparing with certainty today for the uncertainties of tomorrow by telling a story about two houses—one built on the sand, the other built on a rock. Using imagery of rain, wind and storms, Jesus warns that adversity will inevitably come. He didn't say that they *might* come but that they *would* come. He then instructs his listeners that those who hear his teachings and put them into practice, would be like the house built on the rock—the wise ones prepared for the coming storms. In contrast, he warns those who hear the very same teachings but do not put them into practice, would be like the house built on the sand—the foolish ones unprepared for the coming storms. Jesus' main point is that *preparation through practice would determine the difference.*

I learned this same lesson by playing basketball. Although I never really liked to practice, I quickly learned that if I didn't, I wouldn't be any good and as a result, wouldn't get to play. It was that simple. So from elementary school through college, starting in early spring and going through mid-winter, basketball practice was essentially a daily routine for me.

But undoubtedly I learned the most about preparation through practice when I played college basketball. My college coach ended every practice with an endurance drill. He had several wicked ones in his arsenal, but the one I disliked the most was the eleven-wall drill. We had to run the length of the basketball court eleven times, touching the wall at each turn, before the sixty seconds ticking away on the score clock over head ran out. If we didn't finish the drill within the sixty seconds, we had to run the entire drill all over again. Ouch! Even though I despised those drills, I understood the method behind coach's madness; he wanted to build endurance and prepare us for games that were close in the fourth quarter, or games that might go into overtime.

While still exhausted from our endurance drills, we immediately practiced free throws. Coach McElroy assigned each of us a certain number of foul shots that we had to make before we could "hit the showers." Mine was fifteen out of twenty. Again, I understood the purpose of the drill. Coach wanted the correct shooting form so engrained in us—knees bent, elbow in, arm straight, fingers spread, eyes on the back of the rim, ball released next to the ear—so that we would accurately shoot free throws, even when exhausted and under intense pressure at the end of a close game.

Dr. William C. De Vries, who installed the first artificial heart in a human, also understood the need for practice. When asked why he had practiced the same installation procedure hundreds of times in animals before installing the first artificial heart in a human, Dr. De Vries replied, "The reason you practice so much is so that you will do things automatically the same way every time." [1]

Long before Coach McElroy or Dr. De Vries, Jesus taught this same principle. In his story about the two houses his emphasis wasn't about people simply listening, admiring, or being entertained by his teachings. Nor was his emphasis about people dissecting or debating his words for the sole purpose of passing on nice, religious ideas to others. Rather, his emphasis was on *practicing his teachings*—establishing them as daily disciplines resulting in a way of life that could be relied upon during the pressures of life. According to Jesus, when the storms come, preparation through practice would determine which house would be left standing.

Over the years I have watched so many people live life as if storms would never blow their way. Somehow they believe they will be the exception, and sadly, as a result, they don't properly prepare with certainty today for the uncertainties of tomorrow. I've seen this same storyline unfold in so many people's lives that regrettably, I can write the final script years before it fully plays out.

The deception is not only in the denial that storms won't come our way, but the danger is also in the delay of preparing for them. You can't wait until you're in the middle of a storm and then try to prepare. That's like trying to build a house during a hurricane. It's foolish and futile.

I'm grateful and fortunate that over the years, I had heeded the words of Jesus, practiced his teachings, and prepared for the storm that inevitably did come. Years of making the teachings of Jesus a practical part of my daily life before my wife's passing, became the foundation for shaping my thinking, guiding my emotions, and directing my decisions in the days following, and now years since, her passing.

Like my own, my wife's preparation for days of uncertainty had begun in her early years.

Debbie grew up in Northwest Canada in a small town located in the Peace River country, surrounded by expansive wheat farms and booming oil fields. Brutal winters arrived in early November and stayed until late May. At that time, Grand Prairie Alberta still had the flavor of a rough and rugged frontier town. Paved roads were a luxury and beat up trucks a necessity. A moose strolling through town or a close encounter with a bear were as common as the weekend bar room brawls.

It was in this place that my wife, at a very young age, distinctly recalls making a decision to follow Christ. As if it were only yesterday, she would relate to me, with great clarity and fondness, the setting and surroundings of giving her life to Christ. That life changing decision she made as a little girl, would not only determine her final destiny but it would also determine how she would live her life until her death.

Rick Warren, in his book, *A Purpose Driven Life*, challenges all of us to think about our life in the light of death. He writes, "You may feel it's morbid to think about death, but actually it's unhealthy to live in denial of death… Only a fool would go through life unprepared for what we know will eventually happen. You need to think more about eternity, not less… When we fully comprehend that there is more to life than just here and now, and you realize that life is just preparation for eternity, you will begin to live life differently." [2]

Debbie had not only prepared for her death, but as Rick Warren suggests, she lived her life in the awareness of her eventual death. In fact, in the last few years of my wife's life, almost as if she was being prepared for what was to come, a specific Scripture had profoundly gripped her and was affecting how she was living out each and every day of her life. The Scripture was 2 Corinthians 4:16-18.

"Though outwardly we are wasting away, yet inwardly, we are being renewed day by day. For our light and momentary troubles are achieving for us an eternal glory that far outweighs them all. So, we fix our eyes not on what is seen, but on what is unseen. For what is seen is temporary, but what is unseen is eternal."

She would often quote this particular Scripture to me and then mention a decision she had made, or something she had decided to do (or not do) in light of it. Since this Scripture had become so central to the way my wife had lived her life in the years before her death, we printed it on the front of her memorial service program. But it was placed there not as a nice religious idea of what should have been, but as a reality of what her life had been.

A recent review of some files containing several teachings Debbie had shared with women in the church we pastored, only reinforced to me how my wife had been living her life in light of eternity. As I sat on the floor of my home office with the pages of her teachings scattered in front of me, intensely reading each word, I was struck by the power and relevance of her words—words not only to live by, but words to truly die by.

One of the excerpts reads,

How short our lives are, how swiftly time moves on. It seems like yesterday I was pulling my hair out wondering if "toddler hood" would ever be over, and now, with my two children being fifteen and thirteen, I sometimes wish I had those years back. I can honestly say I have no regrets investing my life in my children.

Sometimes you see the rewards of your investments. At other times you don't. Just the other day my husband and I were sitting at the table talking about our lives, when our children commented on how they wanted to have the same kind of faith in God we had. What a compliment. Other things will come and go, but my investment in my children is very significant. It is eternal. Truly, there is a reward that awaits all of us who remain faithful and obedient.

A portion from another one of my wife's teachings read,

If only in this life we have hope in Christ, we are to be pitied more than all men. In other words, if I go through life and have to suffer all these things and there is nothing beyond this life, pity me. It's not worth it. But if I have a guarantee that the life to come will be one without sorrow, tears, pain, hardship, separation—then as I'm going through these very things while on this earth, hope in the life to come is what sustains me. This life is fleeting. But the next life is eternal, without end. That's what I am looking for. That's what I'm waiting for.

In light of what my friend said to me on that fateful Friday afternoon, "No, we can't prepare for times of difficulties in a day, but we can prepare with certainty today for the certain uncertainties of tomorrow."

One of the amazing things I experienced after my wife's passing was the ability to sleep at night. Many people, after going through a tragedy experience tormenting, endless nights. But that wasn't my experience. I went to bed, read for a while and night after night, fell into a deep restful sleep. On the sixteenth night after my wife's death, however something very special occurred as I slept. I had a dream about her.

In my dream Debbie and I were traveling together somewhere in the Deep South. Whether it was New Orleans, Charleston, or Atlanta, it wasn't quite clear but nevertheless, we found ourselves in a picturesque suburb on the outskirts of this large metropolitan area. We were walking through a beautiful neighborhood where magnolia trees in full bloom lined the streets. Lovely plantation homes—complete with white pillars, gorgeous flower gardens, and white picket fences sat on perfectly manicured lawns. The entire neighborhood was an idyllic picture of tranquility and contentment.

Next to this neighborhood was a quaint, upscale shopping area that we decided to explore. As we continued our day, enjoying the sunny afternoon and making our way in and out of the charming boutiques and novelty shops, somehow Debbie and I drifted apart. Initially unconcerned, I continued to browse through the shops thinking I would eventually run into her. But when, after several more minutes I didn't find her, I decided to return to the nearby neighborhood and look for her.

As I strolled by one of the pristine plantation homes, my eyes were drawn to the back of the house, where inside a large glass sunroom I could see a ladies' tea party in progress. Hesitantly, I made my way to the back door of the sunroom and knocked, prepared to ask if anyone had seen my wife.

A pleasant and elegant looking lady in her mid to late 40s opened the door. I explained that I was looking for my wife and asked if she had, by chance, seen her. Although the woman clearly acknowledged me, she didn't say a word. That was strange enough, but what was even more strange was the sense that as she looked at me she wasn't actually looking *at* me, but looking *into* me. All the other ladies at the tea party, nicely dressed and also appearing to be in their 40s and 50s, likewise acknowledged my presence. But again, no one said a word. They just gave me that same pleasant yet penetrating look and then returned to enjoying their party and sipping their tea.

I started to step into the sunroom, but as I did, I felt an odd sensation. Something about this tea party was very unsettling to me. It felt as though I was about to cross an invisible plane and into another world, a world I didn't fully recognize yet somehow intensely longed for. But I turned and quickly walked away, feeling uneasy yet strangely warmed.

By now, as I continued my search for Debbie my pace had quickened. I hurried through the neighborhood frantic to find her and only moments later found myself walking by the same house where the ladies' tea party was still in progress. As I turned and looked toward the house, like someone waving a magic wand, a deep Irish green washed over the lawn, the flower garden exploded into an array of vibrant colors, the house turned a brilliant, pure white, and the sunroom burst into a kaleidoscope of shimmering brightness. Everything was pulsating with life and light. It was as if a magical storybook land had appeared right before my eyes. And then I saw her.

In the middle of the sun room, with the party continuing around her, dressed in a beautiful crimson gown, Debbie stood up. As I peered into the radiant and glowing sunroom, desperately hoping to get her attention, she turned and looked at me and the space between us fell away. Her face was filled with indescribable peace, unimaginable contentment, perfect purity, and overwhelming joy. With her eyes locked on mine, Debbie gave me a warm, radiant, and reassuring smile, as if to say, "Honey, everything is ok. I'm finally home."

Reflection/Discussion Questions

1. Are you preparing with certainty today for the uncertainties of tomorrow? If yes, how? If no, why?

2. Is your house being built upon the rock or upon the sand?

3. Are you living your life today in light of a day of inevitable death?

4. Are you denying the reality of the coming storms of life? And are you delaying in properly preparing for them?

5. Are you prepared to live?

6. Are you prepared to die?

Notes

Chapter Two—Navigating Life

1. Henry David Thoreau, Walden And Other Writings (New York, New York: Random House, 1992), 86.
2. Psalms 86:11: The Message Translation (Colorado Springs, Colorado: NavPress).

Chapter Three—Lingering Questions

1. Ruth Graham, *In Every Pew Sits A Broken Heart* (Grand Rapids, Michigan: Zondervan, 2004), 39.
2. Philip Comfort, *Life Application Commentary on Ephesians* (Carol Streams, Illinois: Tyndale House Publishers Inc., 1996), 59.
3. Dr. Larry Crabb, *Shattered Dreams* (Colorado Springs, Colorado: WaterBrook Press, 2001), 79-80.

Chapter Four—Shattered Dreams

1. Dr. Larry Crabb, *Shattered Dreams* (Colorado Springs, Colorado: WaterBrook Press, 2001), 114.
2. Matthew 19:27: The Message Translation (author's paraphrase).

Chapter Five—Solid Footing

1. Ruth Graham, *In Every Pew Sits A Broken Heart* (Grand Rapids, Michigan: Zondervan, 2004), 107.
2. Dallas Willard, *Renovation Of The Heart* (Colorado Springs, Colorado: NavPress, 2002), 70.
3. Mitch Albom, *Tuesdays with Morrie* (New York, New York: Broadway Books, 1997), 82.
4. Matthew 16:25 & 26 The Amplified New Testament.

Chapter Six—A Costly Life _
1. Ruth Haley Barton, *Sacred Rhythms* (Downers Grove, Illinois: InterVarsity Press, 2006), 9.
2. Dr. Larry Crabb, *Shattered Dreams* (Colorado Springs, Colorado: WaterBrook Press, 2001), 181.

Chapter Seven—Shaped By Life
1. Henry Ward Beecher, *The Brainy Quote Site.*
2. James 1:2-4.
3. Dallas Willard, *Renovation of the Heart* (Colorado Springs, Colorado: NavPress, 2002), 19.
4. Romans 8:29-30 The Message Translation (Colorado Springs, Colorado: NavPress).
5. Galatians 4:19 & Romans 12:2.
6. Matthew Kelly, *The Rhythm of Life* (Steubenville, Ohio: Beacon Publishing, 1999), 43.
7. Dallas Willard, *The Spirit of the Disciplines* (New York, New York: Harper Collins Publishers Inc., 1991), 118.

Chapter Eight—Fight for Life
1. C.S. Lewis, *Mere Christianity* (New York, New York: Harper Collins, 1980), 45.
2. R.C. Sproul, *Pleasing God* (Wheaton, Illinois: Tyndale Publishing, 1988), 88.
3. John 10:10.
4. John Eldredge, *Waking the Dead* (Nashville, Tennessee: Thomas Nelson Publishing, 2003), 13.

Chapter Nine—Looking Up
1. Charles Swindoll, *Dropping Your Guard* (Nashville, Tennessee: Thomas Nelson Publishing, 1988), 192.
2. Ibid., 162.
3. Ibid., 193.

4. Dante Alighieri, *The Divine Comedy*, Translated by John Cairdi (New York, New York: The Penguin Group), 47.
5. David Jacobsen, *Hostage*: Interview on *60 Minutes*.
6. Reggie McNeal, *Practicing Greatness* (San Francisco, CA: Jossey-Bass, 2006), 80.
7. Erwin McManus, *UPRISING: A Revolution Of The Soul* (Nashville, Tennessee: Thomas Nelson, 2003), 13.
8. Bruce Wilkinson, *The Dream Giver* (Sisters, Oregon: Multnomah, 2003), 6.
9. Erwin Mcmanus, *UPRISING: A Revolution Of The Soul* (Nashville, Tennessee: Thomas Nelson Publishers, 2003), 14.
10. Richard Foster, *Seeking the Kingdom* (New York, New York: Harper Collins Publishers, 1995), 102.
11. C.S. Lewis, *The Screwtape Letters* and *Screwtape Proposes A Toast* (New York, New York: Macmillan, 1962), 60, 40.
12. John Piper, *Future Grace* (Sisters, Oregon: Multnomah, 1995), 9.

Chapter Ten—Preparing for Death

1. Dallas Willard, *The Spirit of the Disciplines* (New York, New York: Harper Collins Books, 1988), 153.
2. Rick Warren, *Purpose Driven Life* (Grand Rapids, Michigan: Zondervan, 2002), 37, 39.

Ken Roberts is the visionary leader and primary teaching pastor of New Life Community, located in Maple Grove, Minnesota. Before serving at New Life Community, Ken served for twenty-five years on the pastoral team of Worldview Community Church, located in Olmsted Falls, Ohio.

His ongoing desire is to create a place where authentic Christ-followers can reach their full redemptive potential through the process of spiritual formation and as a result fulfill their God given purposes and passions. Ken's vision is to see an authentic, intergenerational, and missional spiritual community committed to growing from the inside out and as a result having a city, national and global impact.

Ken lives with his wife Missy in Maple Grove, Minnesota. He has three adult children, Nicole and Britton, and a stepson, Mychael.

Unexpected: Navigating Life's Unforeseen Turns is Ken's first book. His second book, ***Shaped by Leading***, written for Christian leaders is currently in process.

To order more books or learn more about the author go to www.KenLRoberts.com

Intermedia
Publishing Group

Publishing That Works For You

Do you need a speaker?

Do you want Ken L. Roberts to speak to your group or event? Then contact Larry Davis at: **(623) 337-8710** or email:
ldavis@intermediapr.com or use the contact form at: **www.intermediapr.com**.

Whether you want to purchase bulk copies of Unexpected or buy another book for a friend,
get it now at:
www.imprbooks.com.

If you have a book that you would like to publish, contact Terry Whalin, Publisher, at Intermedia Publishing Group, (623) 337-8710 or
email: **twhalin@intermediapub.com**
or use the contact form at: **www.intermediapub.com**.